THE SCIENCE FICTION NOVEL
imagination and social criticism

THE SCIENCE

Basil Davenport

Robert A. Heinlein

C. M. Kornbluth

Alfred Bester

Robert Bloch

FICTION NOVEL

imagination

and social criticism

Chicago: 1969

In Memoriam
C. M. Kornbluth

Library of Congress Catalog Card No. 58-7492

International Standard Book Numbers 0-911682-02-3 (cloth)
0-911682-13-9 (paper)

Copyright ©, 1959, by Advent:Publishers

THIRD EDITION, July 1969

CLOTH PRINTINGS: July 1969, April 1971, Sept. 1974
PAPER PRINTINGS: July 1969, Sept. 1970, Oct. 1971, Sept. 1974

CONTENTS

7 BASIL DAVENPORT . . . . introduction

14 ROBERT A. HEINLEIN . . . . . science fiction:
its nature, faults and virtues

49 C. M. KORNBLUTH . . . . . the failure of the
science fiction novel as social criticism

77 ALFRED BESTER . . . . . . science fiction and
the renaissance man

97 ROBERT BLOCH . . . . imagination and
modern social criticism

122 INDEX

BASIL DAVENPORT

introduction

T HE PAPERS WHICH MAKE UP THIS BOOK, BY
four eminent writers in the field of
science fiction, were originally delivered
as lectures at University College in the University of Chicago.
In my Oxford days the colleges there also had the privilege
of lectures by distinguished guests, and one of the speakers
most in demand was Father Ronald Knox (the late Bishop
Knox, famous for his translation of the Bible). I have always
remembered a burlesque talk he gave on the value of a university education. "You will find," he said, "that an Oxford
education is of value in any situation in which you may
find yourselves. For example, suppose that Lady Smith has

opened a bazaar, and you are asked to propose a vote of thanks. You may begin, 'I am called upon to propose a vote of thanks to Lady Smith. When I was at Oxford, we were taught always to define our terms; and so I should say that this depends upon—er—what you mean by thanks, and—er— what you mean by lady.' "

In the same way, what you think about science fiction and social criticism depends on what you mean by science fiction, and what you mean by social criticism. None of our authors attempts to define social criticism, though C. M. Kornbluth limits his discussion to effective social criticism, criticism which produces visible results; and the others consider it as criticism concerned only with social structure, as distinct from social attitudes. (I shall return to these points in a moment.) Only one of our authors, Robert Heinlein, attempts to define science fiction, the other three assume that we shall know what they are talking about. And no doubt that assumption is correct; but when you stop to think of it, it is a remarkable thing that a branch of literature which (as Mr. Heinlein tells us), twenty-five years ago did not even have a name which was generally accepted, is now so well known that it can safely be assumed that a reader will know in general what is meant when it is named—even though it is probable that no two people would agree on precisely the same definition.

If anyone does want a definition of science fiction, there is one to be found at the beginning of Mr. Heinlein's "Science Fiction: Its Nature, Faults and Virtues," which opens this book. His definition is too long to quote here, and too closely reasoned to summarize. It covers the ground admirably— although, to support my statement that no two people would agree on precisely the same definition, I must add that in my opinion he stakes out too wide a claim. A definition of science fiction that can include ghost stories at one extreme and Sinclair Lewis' *Arrowsmith* at the other is almost too indefinite to be a definition, though Mr. Heinlein unquestionably makes out a logical case on his own terms. At the paranormal end of his spectrum, I am sincerely grateful to him for restoring to science fiction (which by most definitions deals with the theoretically possible) the important fields of time travel and travel faster than the speed of light; he points out that these are contrary not to known fact but to accepted theory, a point on which I confess I had myself been confused. But when it comes to including ghosts, my objection is not that they are not possible (without committing myself as to what is their nature, I believe that apparitions of the dead are very nearly established facts), but that they are not scientific, and surely there ought to be some science in science fiction. Time travel must be based on some sort of science, but I do not see how ghost stories can be, unless Mr. Heinlein is willing to admit necromancy as a science. My reasons for excluding *Arrowsmith* are harder to state logically. It is true that a newly discovered cure unknown to medicine today plays a part in the plot, though not a central part. But hang it, *Arrowsmith* doesn't read like science fiction! Let me put it this way: I read *Arrowsmith* when it first came out, which must be more than thirty years ago, when I was young and avid for science fiction and there was very little of it around, and I never suspected that this might be a part of what I was looking for. Surely one cannot read science fiction, as Monsieur Jourdain spoke prose, without knowing it.

But if no two people would agree on precisely the same definition of science fiction, at least three of our contributors are in substantial agreement about science fiction as social criticism. The fourth is Mr. Heinlein, whose treatment of the general subject is highly stimulating, but, like his definition, is hard to pin down on this particular issue. The other three reach the same conclusion, if one may let the cat out of the bag so early, which may be summed up in the title of Mr. Kornbluth's piece, "The Failure of the Science Fiction Novel as Social Criticism." When I found three distinguished authors of science fiction coming to this melancholy agreement, I was reminded of the incident in Isak Dinesen's story "The Deluge at Norderney," when the old grande dame says to the Cardinal, "These are terrible words, my Lord, to the ears of a Legitimist," and he solemnly replies, "What are they, then, to the lips of a Legitimist?" This is a sad and surprising conclusion to me, a mere fan, and must have been even more so to the authors, and though I must agree with them in general, I cannot refrain from putting down a few points in mitigation.

Of the three authors, I imagine that Mr. Bester would find the least to regret in a partial failure of science fiction. He regards the right kind of enjoyment of science fiction as merely one of the minor pleasures of life for the well-rounded Renaissance man. He goes so far as to say, "We can only enjoy it (science fiction) when we're calm and euphoric," i.e., in a state of euphoria; and a moment later he adds, "Only a man who has known adult troubles can know the meaning of euphoria," which would appear to amount to a syllogism proving that no young person can enjoy science fiction. To do him justice, he immediately qualifies this by saying that "Young people often withdraw into unadulterated escape fiction, including science fiction," but, one gathers, this is to enjoy science fiction in the wrong way and for the wrong reason. And similarly, one feels that if Mr. Bester did find any social criticism in science fiction, he would regard it as irrelevant to science fiction's true purpose, which is to be the American equivalent of the pub or the weinstube.

Mr. Kornbluth, far from being satisfied to regard science fiction as a minor pleasure for the Renaissance man, regrets that it has accomplished so little; that "even though science fiction contains a high percentage of explicit and implicit social criticism," it has not yet had the visible social effects of *Don Quixote*, *Uncle Tom's Cabin* and other books which he names. He goes on into some Freudian speculations as to the reason for this, into which I shall not follow him beyond suggesting that he might make his case stronger by exploring certain affinities between science fiction and poetry. But even though it is true that science fiction is still waiting for its *Uncle Tom's Cabin* or even its *Babbitt*, still I should like to urge first that it may have made more difference in social attitudes than can be traced, and second, that prophecies of evil if taken as warnings naturally defeat themselves. In 1903 there appeared a novel, *The Riddle of the Sands*, by Erskine Childers, which I think might rate as science fiction by Mr. Heinlein's definition. It described the uncovering of a German plot to make a sneak invasion of England across the North Sea in a flotilla of flat-bottomed boats. There is a persistent rumor, impossible to prove or disprove, that there actually was such a plot, and that the publication of the book rendered it impracticable. If the worst prophecies of science fiction have not been fulfilled, we may have science fiction partly to thank. Who can say how many people have gained a truer insight into the workings of the totalitarian state from *1984*, or have been more alert to the danger of mind-conditioning since reading *Brave New World*? And Mr. Kornbluth has avowedly limited his field, as of course he has every right to do, to demonstrably effective social criticism. The social criticism in *Gulliver's Travels* is no less trenchant because one cannot definitely trace any reforms to it.

With disturbing cogency, Robert Bloch mounts a real offensive, charging science fiction not merely with being ineffective as social criticism, but with accepting in large part the worst of today's values, including revenge and the justification of violence, and with a failure to come to the help of anything really unpopular. There is a painfully large amount in what he says. By and large, science fiction has been at its least imaginative in inventing alternative societies, especially alternative good societies. In general any society which differs widely from our own is set up only to be overthrown. Thus there is a regular formula which has produced at least half a dozen novels, some of them highly readable and exciting: the world is run by a single organization—a government, a church, a monster business—with ostensible benevolence; the hero is a dedicated young idealist in the service of the organization, believing its pretensions of benevolence, until a beautiful girl revolutionary shows him the seamy side of it, whereupon he changes sides and overthrows it—yes, practically single-handed. And what he sets up instead is always essentially twentieth century American civilization, plus a few added gadgets. Our own society seems to be not only the best, but the only good society that science fiction has been able to conceive. We need to be reminded that there are other possibilities. I will venture the heresy that Aristotle said that there are three possible forms of government: the rule of one, the rule of a few, and the rule of all; and that all three can be either good or bad.

And certainly, we need to be reminded not only that there are other possible good societies, there are conceivably better societies. Science fiction has produced very few Utopias, and those not very imaginative or even tempting; it has done better with Utopias in reverse, but for them, unfortunately, less imagination is needed. The last of the Utopians was H. G. Wells. Down to his time it was still possible to believe, like William Morris and Bellamy, that one could present a picture of the future that was so desirable that people would try to bring it into being; since then, the best hope of Huxley and Orwell has been that they could present the future as so terrifying that we would at least try to avoid it. And even Wells' Utopias, in *Men Like Gods* for instance, were both vague as blueprints and, it always seemed to me, pretty dull as prospects, reminding one of Byron's lines about the Garden of Eden:

> Nothing but birds, and butterflies, and flowers—
> I wonder how they got through the twelve hours!

There certainly exists here a gap to be filled. But it is only recently that science has moved out of the fields of physics and biology into those of the inexact sciences, and let us hope that speculative sociology may be the next province to be invaded. We have at least had one story with an attractive and fairly convincing Utopia based on the principles of Thoreau's *Civil Disobedience*; let us hope for more.

As for defending the unpopular, one of the most striking developments in science fiction since the days of *The War of the Worlds* and *The Skylark of Space* has been the realization that men and Martians need not necessarily exterminate or enslave each other. Story after story of encounters with alien races offers the same lesson, that to be different is not necessarily to be evil. And I can think of at least two stories in which the toleration which we are learning to accord the hypothetical is claimed for homosexuals, those aliens in our midst; one of these stories seems to me the most moving and persuasive plea in that regard that I have ever read.

By the way, to do Mr. Bloch justice, I believe he mentions as an honorable exception a book in which one of these stories occurs. But of course I am not trying to argue with Mr. Bloch, or with the other authors of this book, all of whom have much to say beyond the points which I have chosen for comment. I am afraid I have been committing the unforgivable fault in a toastmaster, saying "You have not come here to listen to me," and then going on to make the speaker's speech for him. My excuse is that I could not help it. This book has given me the pleasure, all too rare since my college days, of being a book that I could argue with. No one can agree with all these papers, since they do not agree with each other; but where you disagree you will find yourself wanting to say exactly how far and why. That is my idea of a really stimulating and enjoyable book.

ROBERT A. HEINLEIN

science fiction:
its nature, faults and virtues

FIRST LET US DECIDE WHAT WE MEAN BY THE term "science fiction"—or at least what we will mean by it here. Anyone wishing a scholarly discussion of the etymology of the term will find one by Sam Moskowitz in the February, 1957, issue of *The Magazine of Fantasy and Science Fiction.* I shan't repeat what he has said so well but will summarize for our immediate purposes. The field now known as science fiction had no agreed name until about twenty-five years ago. The field has existed throughout the history of literature but it used to be called by several names: speculative romance,

* Based on a lecture delivered February 8, 1957, University College, The University of Chicago. Copyright, 1959, by Robert A. Heinlein.

pseudo-scientific romance (a term that sets a science fiction writer's teeth on edge), utopian literature, fantasy—or, more frequently, given no name, simply lumped in with all other fiction.

But the term "science fiction" is now part of the language, as common as the neologism "guided missile." We are stuck with it and I will use it . . . although personally I prefer the term "speculative fiction" as being more descriptive. I will use these two terms interchangeably, one being the common handle, the other being one that aids me in thinking—but with the same referent in each case.

"Science fiction" means different things to different people. "When I make a word do a lot of work like that," said Humpty Dumpty, "I always pay it extra"—in which case the term science fiction has piled up a lot of expensive overtime. Damon Knight, a distinguished critic in this field, argues that there is no clear distinction between fantasy and science fiction, in which opinion August Derleth seems to agree. I cannot forcefully disagree with their lines of reasoning—but I wonder if they have made their definitions so broad as to include practically all fiction? To define is to limit; a definition cannot be useful unless it limits. Certainly Mickey Spillane's murder stories could easily be classed as fantasies, as can many or most of the love stories appearing in the big slick magazines. But I feel sure that Mr. Knight and Mr. Derleth did not intend their definitions to be quite that unbounded and in any case my difference of opinion with them is merely a matter of taste and personal convenience.

Theodore Sturgeon, a giant in this field, defines a science fiction story as one in which the story would not exist if it were not for the scientific element—an admirably sharp delimitation but one which seems to me perhaps as uncomfortably tight as the one above seems to me unusefully roomy. It would exclude from the category "science fiction" much of Mr. Sturgeon's best work, stories which are to my mind speculative rather than fantastic. There are many stories that are lumped into the class "science fiction" in the minds of most people (and in mine) which contain only a detectable trace, or none, of science—for example, Sinclair Lewis' *It Can't Happen Here*, Fritz Leiber's great short story "Coming Attraction," Thomas F. Tweed's novel *Gabriel Over the White House*. All three stories are of manners and morals; any science in them is merely parsley trimming, not the meat. Yet each is major speculation, not fantasy, and each must be classed as science fiction as the term is commonly used.

Reginald Bretnor, author, editor and acute critic of this field, gives what is to me the most thoughtful, best reasoned, and most useful definition of science fiction. He sees it as a field of literature much broader than that often termed "main-stream" literature — or "non-science fiction," if you please—science fiction being that sort in which the author shows awareness of the nature and importance of the human activity known as the scientific method, shows equal awareness of the great body of human knowledge already collected through that activity, and takes into account in his stories the effects and possible future effects on human beings of scientific method and scientific fact. This indispensable three-fold awareness does not limit the science fiction author to stories about science—he need not write a gadget story; indeed a gadget story would not be science fiction under this definition if the author failed in this three-fold awareness. Any subject can be used in a science fiction story under this definition, provided (and indispensably required) that the author has the attitude comprised by the three-fold awareness and further provided that he has and uses appropriately that body of knowledge pertinent to the scope of his story. I have paraphrased in summary Mr. Bretnor's comments and I hope he will forgive me.

Mr. Bretnor's definition gives the science fiction author almost unlimited freedom in subject matter while requiring of him high, rigorous, difficult and mature standards in execution.

In contrast to science fiction thus defined, non-science fiction—all other fiction including the most highly acclaimed "literary" novels—at most shows awareness of the by-products of scientific method already in existence. Non-science fiction admits the existence of the automobile, radar, polio vaccine, H-bombs, etc., but refuses to countenance starships and other such frivolities. That is to say, non-science fiction will concede that water is running down hill but refuses to admit that it might ever reach the bottom . . . or could ever be pumped up again. It is a static attitude, an assumption that what is now forever shall be.

An example of the great scope of this definition is Sinclair Lewis' novel *Arrowsmith*, a story motivated by the human problems of a man aware of and consciously trying to practice the scientific method in medical research in the face of difficulties. *Arrowsmith* was not labeled science fiction by its publisher, it is not concerned with space ships nor the year 3000; nevertheless it is science fiction at its best, it shows that three-fold awareness to the utmost and is a rousin' good yarn of great literary merit.

Let's back off for a moment and compare science fiction with other forms of fiction. First: what is fiction?

Merriam-Webster: "Works of imagination in narrative form."

Funk & Wagnalls: "Imaginary narrative."

Thorndike-Barnhart: "Prose writings about imaginary people and happenings."

Fowler's *Modern English Usage* equates "fictitious" with "imaginary."

These reasonably equivalent definitions are all based on the common element "imaginary"—so let's put it in everyday words: Fiction is storytelling about imaginary things and people. These imaginary tales are usually intended to entertain and sometimes do, they are sometimes intended to instruct and occasionally manage even that, but the only element common to all fiction is that all of it deals with imaginary events. Even fiction of the most sordid and detailed ash-can realism is imaginary—or it cannot be termed fiction.

But if all fiction is imaginary, how is realistic fiction to be distinguished from fantasy?

The lexicographers cited above are not quite so unanimous here. However, I find certain words used over and over again in their discussions of fantasy: "dream, caprice, whim, fanciful, conceit, figment, unreal, irrational." These descriptive words have a common element; they all imply imaginings which are not limited by the physical universe as we conceive it to be.

I therefore propose to define "fantasy" in accordance with the implication common to the remarks of these lexicographers. There have been many wordy and fruitless battles over the exact meaning of the word "fantasy"; I have no intention of starting another. I ask merely that you accept for the purpose of better communication during the balance of this essay a definition based on the above. When I say "fantasy fiction" I shall mean "imaginary-and-not-possible" in the world as we know it; conversely all fiction which I regard as "imaginary-but-possible" I shall refer to as "realistic fiction," i.e., imaginary but could be real so far as we know the real universe.

Science fiction is in the latter class. It is not fantasy.

I am not condemning fantasy, I am defining it. It has greater freedom than any other form of fiction, for it is completely independent of the real world and is limited only by literary rules relating to empathy, inner logic and the like. Its great freedom makes it, in the hands of a skilled craftsman, a powerful tool for entertainment and instruction— humor, satire, gothic horror, anything you wish. But a story is not fantasy simply because it deals with the strange, the exotic, the horrible, the unusual or the improbable; both fantasy and realistic fiction may have any of these elements. It is mere provincialism to confuse the wildly strange with fantasy; a fantasy story is one which denies in its premise some feature of the real world, it may be quite humdrum in all other respects, e.g., Eric Knight's *The Flying Yorkshireman*.

Conversely, a realistic story may be wildly strange while holding firmly to the possibilities of the real world — e.g., E. E. Smith's *Gray Lensman*. The science fiction author is not limited by currently accepted theory nor by popular opinion; he need only respect established fact.

Unfortunately there is never full agreement as to the "established facts" nor as to what constitutes the "real world," and definitions by intention are seldom satisfactory. By these two terms I mean the factual universe of our experience in the sense in which one would expect such words to be used by educated and enlightened members of the western culture in 1959.

Even this definition contains semantic and philosophic difficulties but I shall not attempt to cope with them in this limited space; I will limit myself to pointing out some stories which, in my opinion, deny some essential fact of the real world and therefore are, by the "imaginary-and-not-possible" definition, fantasy:

My story *Magic, Inc.*; E. R. Eddison's *The Worm Ouroboros*; the Oz books; stories using talking mules, or Seacoast Bohemia, or astrology treated as if it were a science; any story based on violation of scientific fact, such as space ship stories which ignore ballistics, stories which have the lizard men of Zlxxt crossbreeding with human females, stories which represent the surface conditions of Mars as being much like those of Earth. Let me emphasize: Assumptions contrary to fact such as the last one mentioned do not in themselves invalidate a story; C. S. Lewis' powerful *Out of the Silent Planet* is not spoiled thereby as a religious parable—it simply happens to be fantasy rather than science fiction.

Very well—from here on "fantasy" will be considered identically equal to "impossible story."

All other fiction including science fiction falls into the category "imaginary-but-possible." Examples: Frederic Wakeman's *The Hucksters*, Dr. E. E. Smith's galactic romances, Daniel Defoe's *Moll Flanders*; stories about time travel, other dimensions, speeds faster than light, extra-sensory perception; many ghost stories, ones about extra-terrestrial life, John Steinbeck's *The Grapes of Wrath*.

You will have noted that I make the category "possible" very broad. Faster-than-light, time travel, reincarnation, ghosts, all these may strike some of you as impossible, contrary to scientific fact. No, they are contrary to present orthodox theory only and the distinction is extremely important. Such stories may be invalidated by their treatments; they cannot be ruled out today as impossible simply because of such themes. Speeds faster than light would seem to be excluded by Einsteinian theory, a theory which has stood up favorably under many tests, but such an exclusion would be a subjective one, as anyone may see by examining the equations; furthermore, Dr. Einstein's theories and related ones are now being subjected to careful re-examination; the outcome is not yet. As for time travel, we know almost nothing about the nature of time; anyone who has his mind made up either pro or con about time travel is confusing his inner opinions with objective reality. We simply don't know.

With respect to reincarnation, ghosts, ESP and many related matters concerning consciousness, the evidence concerning each is, in 1959, incomplete and in many respects unsatisfactory. We don't even know how consciousness anchors itself to mass; we are short on solid facts in this field and any opinion, positive or negative, can be no better than a tentative hypothesis today.

Hypotheses and theories are always expendable; a scientist modifies or discards them in the face of new facts as casually as he changes his socks. Ordinarily a scientist will use the convenient rule-of-thumb called "least hypothesis" but he owes it no allegiance; his one fixed loyalty is to the observed fact. An honest science fiction writer observes the same loyalty to fact but from there on his path diverges from that of the scientist because his function is different. The pragmatic rule of least hypothesis, useful as it may be to orderly research, is as unfunctional in speculative fiction as a chaperone on a honeymoon. In matters incompletely explored such as reincarnation and time travel the science fiction writer need not be and should not be bound either by contemporary opinion or least hypothesis; his function is to speculate from such facts as there are and to do so as grandly and sweepingly as his imagination permits. He cannot carry out his function while paying lip service to the orthodox opinions or prejudices of his tribe and generation, and no one should expect it of him. It is difficult enough for him to bear in mind a multitude of facts and not wander inadvertently across into fantasy.

I have made perhaps too much of this point because it is a sore one with all science fiction writers; we are regularly charged with "violating facts" when all we have done is to disregard currently respected theory. Every new speculation necessarily starts by kicking aside some older theory.

To categorizing there is no end, and the field of prose fiction may be classified in many different ways: by length, plot, subject, period, locale, language, narrative technique; or by intent—satire, romance, burlesque, comedy, tragedy, propaganda. All these classes blend together and what categories a critic chooses to define depend upon his purpose.

We have divided fiction into possible and impossible; now let us divide again by temporal scene:

REALISTIC FICTION

1. Historical Fiction
2. Contemporary-Scene Fiction
3. Realistic Future-Scene Fiction

FANTASY FICTION

I.   Fantasy laid in the past
II. Fantasy laid in the present
III. Fantasy laid in the future

This arbitrary classification has advantages; on inspecting it several facts show up at once:

So-called "main-stream" literature fills most of class 1 and class 2.

Class 3 contains only science fiction; a small amount of science fiction may also be found in class 1 and class 2.

In the second division, good fantasy, consciously written and skillfully executed, may be found in all three classes. But a great quantity of fake "science" fiction, actually pseudo-scientific fantasy, will be found there also, especially in class III, which is choked with it.

But the most significant fact shining out from the above method of classifying is that class 3, realistic future-scene fiction, contains nothing which is not science fiction and contains at least 90% of all science fiction in print. A handy short definition of almost all science fiction might read: realistic speculation about possible future events, based solidly on adequate knowledge of the real world, past and present, and on a thorough understanding of the nature and significance of the scientific method.

To make this definition cover all science fiction (instead of "almost all") it is necessary only to strike out the word "future." But in fact most science fiction is laid in the future; the reasons for this are not trivial and will be discussed later.

As always, categories tend to overlap, or stories turn out to overlap the categories. We will not offer them Procrustean hospitality—a story is what it is, regardless of a critic's classifications. John Taine's novel *The Time Stream* is science fiction which spans past, present and future; Dr. Frank G. Slaughter's *Sangaree* is a fine historical novel which is also a science fiction novel; Lion Feuchtwanger's *Success* is an historical novel laid in the present and told as if the narrator were in the future; Maxwell Griffith's *The Gadget Maker*, Philip Wylie's *Tomorrow* and Pat Frank's *Forbidden Area* are examples of science fiction laid in a future no later than tomorrow morning. Some stories are such exotic creatures as to defy almost any method of literary taxonomy. A skillful writer could combine in one story an element of fantasy, some of science fiction, a contemporary story, an historical and a bit of the future, some comedy, some tragedy, some burlesque and a little straight hortatory propaganda—in fact I have seen one which includes all of these elements: Vincent McHugh's *Caleb Catlum's America*.

But realistic speculation—science fiction—is usually laid in the future, because it extrapolates from "what is" to "what might be." Some will say that this is the rankest form of fantasy, since the future is not "real." I deny that. We have the dead past, the dying moment and the ever-emerging, always-living future. Our lives always lie in the future; a casual decision to scratch oneself must be carried out at least an instant in the future. The future is all that we can change— and thank Heaven we can!—for the present has obvious shortcomings.

If the future were not real, no insurance company could stay in business. All our lives we are more deeply concerned with what we are going to do than with what we are now doing or have done. The poet who said that every child is the hope of the world understood that. This process is time-binding, the most human of all activities, observing the past in order to make plans for the future. This is the scientific method itself and is the activity which most greatly distinguishes man from other animals. To be able to grasp and embrace the future is to be human.

For this reason I must assert that speculative fiction is much more realistic than is most historical and contemporary-scene fiction and is superior to them both.

Are the speculations of science fiction prophecy? No.

On the other hand, science fiction is often prophetic. There was once a race track tout who touted every horse in each race, each horse to a different sucker. Inevitably he had a winner in every race—he had extrapolated every possibility. Science fiction writers have "prophesied" (if you will excuse a deliberate misuse of the word) so many things and so many possible futures that some of them must come true, with sometimes rather startling accuracy. Having bet on all the horses we can't lose. But much has been made of the "successful prophecies" of science fiction—the electric light, the telephone, the airplane, the submarine, the periscope, tanks, flamethrowers, A-bombs, television, the automobile, guided missiles, robot aircraft, totalitarian government, radar—the list is endless.

The fact is that most so-called "successful prophecies" are made by writers who follow the current scientific reports and indulge in rather obvious extrapolation of already known fact. Let me pick to pieces two cases which I know well because the "prophecies" are attributed to me. The first is from my story *Waldo*, and refers to remote-control manipulators described therein which I called "waldos" after the fictional inventor. Willy Ley calls this "one of the neatest predictions ever to come out of science fiction" and goes on to describe how nearly perfectly I had described the remote-control manipulators now used in atomic "hot" laboratories, even to the use of stereotelevision to conn them . . . even to the development of master and slave teams to permit one operator to do multiple tasks. Sounds pretty good, eh? Especially as the word "waldo" has since become engineering slang.

The second refers to my story "Solution Unsatisfactory." John W. Campbell, Jr., in an essay on this point, lists nine major prophecies in this story, seven of which he says have come true, and two of which, he notes, may very well come true soon. All of them refer to atomic weapons and their impact on history. I might even add that one of those predictions would have come true even more precisely had I not just finished writing another story on atomic power and wished to avoid repeating one of the incidents in it. All of these so-called prophecies were made early in 1940 and they have "come true," so to speak, during the ensuing 19 years.

Sounds as if I own a crystal ball, doesn't it?

Now to pick them to pieces, the latter one first. At the time I wrote "Solution Unsatisfactory" there wasn't enough U-235 in pure state to blow the hat off a flea. But I had had my attention called to its explosive and military possibilities not only by technical reports but both by Mr. Campbell himself (who had maintained his connections at MIT) and by Dr. Robert Cornog, atomic physicist from Berkeley who later helped develop the atomic bomb. Thus I had first hand and most recent scientific knowledge to build on—all this was before security restrictions were placed on the matter, before the famous first pile was erected at the University of Chicago.

I had two more all-important data: a great world war was already going on, and the basic knowledge which made U-235 potentially an unbeatable weapon which could win that war was already known to scientists the world around—even though the public was unaware of it.

Given all this mass of fact could a careful fictionist fail

to come up with something near the truth? As prophecies, those fictional predictions of mine were about as startling as for a man to look out a train window, see that another train is coming head-on toward his own on the same track—and predict a train wreck.

The other one, the waldos or remote control manipulators, was even simpler. Back in 1918 I read an article in *Popular Mechanics* about a poor fellow afflicted with myesthenia gravis, pathological muscular weakness so great that even handling a knife and fork is too much effort. In this condition the brain and the control system are okay, the muscles almost incapable. This man—I don't even know his name; the article is lost in the dim corridors of time—this genius did not let myesthenia gravis defeat him. He devised complicated lever arrangements to enable him to use what little strength he had and he became an inventor and industrial engineer, specializing in how to get maximum result for least effort. He turned his affliction into an asset.

Twenty-two years after I had read about his inspiring example I was scratching my head for a story notion—and I recalled this genius. Now I myself am a mechanical engineer who once specialized in mechanical linkages and had worked in industrial engineering. Is it surprising that with so much real fact to go on and with my own technical background I could describe fictionally remote-control manipulators—"waldos"—which would multiply human muscle power and at the same time handle things with delicate precision? Television had already been invented years before—about twenty years before the public got it—and somebody had already built such linkages, even though they were not in common use. So I "prophesied" them—twenty years after the fact.

What I did miss was that the development of atomics would make waldos utterly indispensable; I predicted them for straight industrial use—now even that is coming true as industry is finding other uses for the manipulators developed for atomics.

But as a "prophecy" I was taking as much chance as a man who predicts tomorrow's sunrise.

These manipulators exist in the opposite direction, too— down into the very small . . . micromanipulators for microchemistry and microsurgery. I have never worked with such things but I learned their details from my wife, who is a microchemist and microsurgeon. Working with such and using a stereomicroscope a skilled operator can excise a living nucleus from a living cell, transplant it to another cell, and cause it to live—a powerful tool in biological research . . . and a beautiful example of research scientist and engineer working together to produce something new. The scientist wanted it—working under his direction, optician and mechanical engineer could make what he needed.

There are other obvious extrapolations from these facts. Put these four things together, the remote-control manipulator with the micromanipulator, television with microscopy. Use micromanipulation to make still smaller instruments which in turn are used to make ones smaller yet. What do you get? A scientist, working safely outside a "hot" laboratory—perhaps with the actual working theater as far away as the Antarctic while the scientist sits in Chicago—seeing by stereomicroscopic television, using remote-control microscopic manipulation, operating not just on a cell and a nucleus, but sorting the mighty molecules of the genes, to determine the exact genetic effect of mutation caused by radiation. Or a dozen other things.

I give this prediction about twenty years, more or less. The basic facts are all in and soon we'll be needing such a technique. There may be a story in it for me, too—another easy dollar as a fake prophet. I'm afraid the itch to prophesy becomes a vice. Forgive me.

Sometimes the so-called prophecies are even less prophetic

than these two I have just deflated. For example, in one story I described a rather remarkable oleo-gear arrangement for handling exceedingly heavy loads. I was not cheating, the device would work; it had been patented about 1900 and has been in industrial use ever since. But it is a gadget not well known to the public and it happened to fit into a story I was writing.

Most so-called science fiction prophecies require very little use of a crystal ball; they are much more like the observations of a man who is looking out a train window rather than down at his lap—he sees the other train coming, and the ensuing "prophecy" is somewhat less remarkable than a lunar eclipse prediction.

However, science and science fiction do interact. There are close relationships between scientists and science fiction writers—indeed some of them are both. H. G. Wells had a degree in biology and kept up with science all his life. Jules Verne worked very closely with scientists. Dr. E. E. Smith is a chemist, a chemical engineer, and a metallurgist. "Philip Latham" is a world-famous astrophysicist. Philip Wylie has a degree in physics, as has "Don A. Stuart." "Murray Leinster" is a chemist. Dr. Isaac Asimov teaches at the medical school of Boston University, does research in cancer, writes college textbooks on biochemistry, writes a junior series of science books as well—and somehow finds time to be a leading science fiction author. "John Taine" is the pen name of one of the ten greatest living mathematicians. L. Sprague de Camp holds three technical degrees. "Lee Correy" is a senior rocket engineer. George O. Smith is a prominent electronics engineer. Chad Oliver is an anthropologist. Is it surprising that such men, writing fiction about what they know best, manage to be right rather often?

But science fiction not infrequently guides the direction of science. I had a completely imaginary electronics device in a story published in 1939. A classmate of mine, then directing such research, took it to his civilian chief engineer and asked if it could possibly be done. The researcher replied, "Mmm . . . no, I don't think so—uh, wait a minute . . . well, yes, maybe. We'll try."

The bread-boarded first model was being tried out aboard ship before the next installment of my story hit the news-stands. The final development of this gadget was in use all through World War II. I wasn't predicting anything and had no reason to think that it would work; I was just dreaming up a gadget to fill a need in a story, sticking as close to fact and possibility as I could.

"Tout ce qu'un homme est capable d'imaginer, d'autres hommes seront capable de la réaliser." (M. Jules Verne—I am indebted to Willy Ley for the quotation.) "Anything one man can imagine, other men can make real." Or to put it in the words of Colonel Turner, first commanding officer of White Sands: "I'll go this far: anything we want to do, we now can do, if we want to badly enough." As Oscar Wilde put it, "Nature mirrors art," . . . and it often does, in science fiction. If a writer knows that mankind wants to do some-thing or needs to do something and that writer is reasonably familiar with current trends in research and development, it is not too hard for him to predict approximately what one of the solutions will be.

However, "in science fiction as in law, ignorance is no excuse," to quote L. Sprague de Camp: The man who has neglected to keep himself informed concerning the frontiers of science, or, even having managed that, fails to be reason-ably knowledgeable about any field of human activity affect-ing his story, or who lacks a fair knowledge of history and current events—failing in any of these things, he has no business writing speculative fiction. It is not enough to inter-lard an old plot with terms like "space warp," "matter trans-mitter," "ray gun," or "rocket ship" with no knowledge of what is meant (if anything) by such terms, or how they might reasonably work. A man who provides Mars with a dense atmosphere and an agreeable climate, a man whose writing shows that he knows nothing of ballistics nor of astronomy nor of any modern technology would do better not to attempt science fiction. Such things are not science fiction—entertainment they may be; serious speculation they cannot be. The obligation of the writer to his reader to know what he is talking about is even stronger in science fiction than elsewhere, because the ordinary reader has less chance to catch him out. It's not fair, it's cheating.

Let's cite another example of the strong interconnection between true science fiction and scientific development itself. Back in 1931 a story by Edmond Hamilton was published called "The Sargasso of Space" which portrayed the first space suits I happen to be aware of. In 1939 I wrote a story, "Misfit," which made much use of space suits, and I remembered how Hamilton had visualized them—remembered with approval—I had done a little suit diving and had some knowledge of engineering and it seemed to me that Hamilton had a good idea; my space suits were elaborated versions of his. A former shipmate of mine, now Rear Admiral A. B. Scoles, was then engaged in aviation research and development. A long-time science fiction fan, Scoles read my story. When we got into the war he sent for me, put me in charge of a high-altitude laboratory of which one of the projects was the development of a space suit (then called a high-altitude pressure suit). I worked on it a short while, then was relieved by L. Sprague de Camp, who is an aeronautical and mechanical engineer as well as a writer; he carried on with this research all through the war, testing and developing many space suits. The war ended; I wrote a story involving space suits in which I applied what I had had opportunity to learn. The story eventually was made into a motion picture, so I sent for a photograph of one of the space suits Sprague de Camp had helped develop, and we copied it as closely as we could for the movie.

With this crossing back and forth between fiction and technology is it surprising that the present-day space suit (or high-altitude pressure suit, if you prefer) now used by the U. S. Air Force strongly resembles in appearance and behavior the space suit visualized by Edmond Hamilton in 1931?

A more startling example of the crossing back and forth between science fiction and technology occurs in space travel itself. I shall not go into it in detail as Arthur C. Clarke, the distinguished science fiction writer and scientist, has already done so—but I will mention some of the pioneers in rocketry who also have written fiction about the subject: Professor Hermann Oberth, Willy Ley, Wernher von Braun, Arthur C. Clarke, G. Harry Stine. This is by no means a complete list; it is illustrative only, and I use it to preface a quotation. I am indebted to Reginald Bretnor for this item; he found it in the pages of America's best known and possibly most respected journal of literary criticism:

"Even before the German inventors created the first navigable rocket at Peenemünde the writers of this somewhat crude form of entertainment had developed the rocket ships which cruised to the moon and the solar planets and then burst into outermost space and explored the galaxies of the Milky Way. Driven by atomic power these apparently mad devices were as well known to the devotees of science fiction as the liners that cross our oceans. Nevertheless, it (space travel) remained unadulterated fantasy until scientists contemplated the experiments with rockets that have proceeded since the last war." *

And this entire quotation is unadulterated tosh!

In literary criticism, as in science fiction and in law, ignorance is no excuse. Let's take it bit by bit:

* *The Saturday Review*, July 17, 1952: "Escape Into Space" (editorial) by "H. S.," presumably Harrison Smith.

"—the German inventors created the first navigable rocket at Peenemünde—" The V-2 was not a navigable rocket; the first navigable rocket was developed in the United States long years after Peenemünde was destroyed.

"—this somewhat crude form of entertainment—" This critic is speaking of the writings of, among others, Dr. Olaf Stapledon, H. G. Wells, Jules Verne, C. S. Lewis, Philip Wylie, Edward Everett Hale, Johannes Kepler, Lucian of Samosata, Cyrano de Bergerac, Edgar Allan Poe. I readily concede that many stories about space travel are crude—but is there any field of literature in which most efforts are not crude? Take a look at any newsstand, any book stall. Is the literary worth of the historical novel *Quo Vadis* gauged by the merits of dime novels and nickel shockers which purport to describe American history?

The examples I have given are a few of the writers of some claim to literary reputation who wrote about space travel prior to the time the first V-2 from Peenemünde fell on London. I submit that a critic who refers to Poe, Wells, Edward Everett Hale, *et al.*, as writers of a "somewhat crude form of entertainment" is spiritually akin to the Hollywood producer who is alleged to have condemned *Hamlet* as "just a moldy old plot strung together with a bunch of familiar quotations." This critic really should familiarize himself with the literature he claims to be judging.

Let us see if he knows any more about science than he appears to know about literature. "—rocket ships which . . . burst into outermost space and explored the galaxies of the Milky Way—"

Any science fiction writer (and almost any twelve-year-old boy) knows that rocket ships are not appropriate for interstellar travel. Obviously this man knows nothing of rocket engineering . . . but his notions of astronomy are even more disheartening. "Galaxies of the Milky Way" indeed! This is about as mixed up concerning the elementary facts of descriptive astronomy as one can get. One could as reasonably call London a borough of New York. I won't take up your time setting him straight; instead I refer him to any Boy Scout.

We are not through with him. "—these apparently mad devices—" Dear literary critic, the telephone is a "mad device" to a Congo pigmy and flying machines were "apparently mad devices" to ignorant minds in the early part of this century.

"—remained unadulterated fantasy until scientists contemplated the experiments with rockets that have proceeded since the last war."

This is so filled with nonsense that I must take it to pieces almost word by word. In the first place, why does he pick this date (around 1944 or '45; he's vague though emphatic) as being the date on which space travel ceased to be "unadulterated fantasy"? Surely not because space travel has already been achieved, for it has not been. But, while space travel is as certain as anything in the future can be, it is not yet here.

In the second place, this critic seems totally unaware that many of the fiction writers about space travel and many of the rocket experimenters who are the true space travel pioneers are, in many important instances, the very same people.

In the third place, he seems just as totally innocent of the history of rocketry—he seems to think that it started at Peenemünde sometime during World War II. Rockets as military missiles (which is what they still are today) date with certainty back through the 18th century and their actual first use is lost in the mists of Chinese history. Mathematical investigation of the problems of space travel and rocketry, and experimentation with rocket prototypes consciously intended to be developed into space ships, both began early in this century. The basic mathematical physics on which a reaction-propelled vehicle capable of moving itself through airless space depends has been available to any educated man since Sir Isaac Newton published his famous Third Law of Motion nearly three hundred years ago. Yet this person seems not even aware of the pioneer work of Professor Oberth and our own Dr. Goddard.

The progress toward space travel has been unbroken and the basic knowledge underlying it has been available to anyone for almost three centuries. The imminence of space travel has been staring in the face of anyone who can read for at least thirty years. I submit that a man who can label all that has gone before as "unadulterated fantasy" is logically as likely so to label any research and development project, in progress but not completed, at Bell Laboratories or Westinghouse. Progress is always accompanied by the wiseacres who stand sneering on the sidelines, always unbelieving before the fact and always without wonder after the fact.

If one were to inflate a toy balloon, release it and allow it to flutter to a stop . . . . There it is, ladies and gentlemen— the self-contained, reaction-propelled vehicle, the prototype of the space ship . . . known to mathematical physics since the time of Newton and now being realized on the drawing boards and in the proving grounds of our fabulously science fictional nation. Yet to ignorant and unimaginative critics it is just a child's balloon. There are none so blind as they who will not see.

Yet this is precisely the sort of "literary criticism" to which science fiction is all too often subjected. I have quoted a gross but not outstanding example.

But what is the literary merit of speculative fiction? By what standards should it be judged?

By precisely the same standards which apply to any other field of fiction. I myself prefer fiction which is entertaining, although some critics do not seem to care about this point. Rules of unity, plot structure, characterization, consistency and all other rules which may fairly be applied to any piece of fiction also should be applied to science fiction; it is not exempt from any of them. It is also subject to another rule which I can best explain by analogy with respect to contemporary-scene fiction and historical fiction. If a man does a story about the packing industry of Chicago, as Upton Sinclair did in *The Jungle*, he owes it to the public first to study the packing industry carefully. If a man writes a novel about Henry VIII he is obligated to know 16th century England as well as he knows his own back yard—and by the same token a man writing about rocket ships is morally obligated to the public to be up on rocket engineering. Since a science fiction writer cannot possibly know all about anthropology, law, history, cybernetics, biochemistry, psychology, mathematics, nucleonics, ballistics and four dozen more major subjects, he is obligated to do just as a competent historical novelist does—make good use of public libraries and other reference sources and seek the advice and help of specialist experts in the fields he touches on. The science fiction writer is especially obligated to do this because many of the subjects he treats are even more esoteric to the average reader than are the facts of 16th century England. Furthermore, his task is both more crucial and more difficult because he is extrapolating, speculating. The historical novelist has a solid and readily accessible framework of known fact to fall back on; the man who speculates about the future has only his knowledge and his reason to guide him.

In other words, all the usual criteria of literature apply to science fiction . . . only more severely.

But, by the same token, I think we who practice it are entitled to be judged only by critics well enough educated to be capable of judging. I do not think that a critic who takes his profession seriously would attempt to judge a novel about Henry VIII without knowing something or learning something of the historical background. At least he should not. But apparently almost any bloke who can read without moving his lips considers himself qualified to take a roundhouse swipe at a speculative novel.

How well does the field of speculative fiction measure up to these conventional literary standards?

Not very well, I am afraid, in most cases. However, there are extenuating circumstances and the accused now throws himself on the mercy of the court. A goodly number of us who write it have had no formal training in writing; we are self-taught and the fact often shows. Regrettably, not too many people have both extensive scientific training and intensive literary training—and good speculative fiction calls for both. However, many excellent writers in many fields have been self-taught; this alone is not sufficient excuse.

A second and more important extenuating circumstance is that speculative fiction is the most difficult of all prose forms. Not only does it require greater knowledge to do it well, greater imagination to make it rational and consistent—these are not easy; almost anyone can write at least one autobiographical novel fairly well; he knows his material, life itself has shaped its consistency and the editor will prune the surplusage—good speculation comes harder. But also, a speculative novel, to be entertaining, must accomplish something which is necessary to all fiction but which is technically very much more difficult in science fiction, i.e., a writer must create the scene and the culture and make it come alive. In historical and contemporary-scene fiction the writer is greatly assisted in this by the fact that the reader is already somewhat familiar with the scene, either through personal experience or through common reading. The speculative story, laid in the future, or on another planet, or possibly in another dimension, cannot use this convenient assumption. The science fiction writer must build up a scene strange to the reader, perhaps a wholly new culture, and he must make it convincing, else he will not simply lose empathy with his reader, he will never gain it in the first place—and there is nothing more dead than a story in which the writer fails to bring his reader into that feeling of belief.

A writer of Western stories may say, "The lone rider topped the rise—spingow!—a shot rang out." Trite perhaps, but the reader knows where he is; he's been there a hundred times before. An historical writer may say: "General Washington stepped outside his headquarters and gazed sadly at the ragged figure of a gaunt private soldier standing barefoot in the snow"—rather trite again, but we know where we are—Valley Forge.

But it is not enough to say, "With a blast the space ship took off for Mars." Oh, it may do for comic books and for pulp magazines aimed at ten-year-olds, but not for serious literature; the writer must fill in this strange scene clearly enough to create empathy.

It's not easy. In the first place he must do it without slowing up the story; neither reader nor literary critic can be expected to hold still for long engineering discussions, or tedious sociological sermonizing. He must get his gadgets in, if he is using gadgets, without getting them in the way of his human characters and their human problems—yet get them in he must, else the story takes place in a literary vacuum and suffocates at once.

This is much harder than the other difficult problems of finding time to do adequate research and then blending that research into a consistent human story. But it must be solved; it is a sine qua non in any story involving a strange scene— the scene and all necessary postulates of the story must be made convincing without cluttering up the story. I will not attempt to explain how to do it; I have been studying the problem by trial and error for years and it still gives me headaches with each new story I write.

This difficulty alone is sufficient to account for the fact that there are very few really good science fiction short stories—solving this problem usually calls for more elbow room than a short story allows. Most short science fiction stories are aimed at the regular reader of the field who has learned to accept certain short-hand assumptions unfamiliar to the general reader (just as the regular reader of the "Western" accepts a complex of assumptions about the American Old West). The valid science fiction short story acceptable to the general reader is not an impossible art form, but it is so excruciatingly difficult that it is quite rare.

But the primary reason that there is so little good science fiction is that there is so little science fiction of any sort.

This may sound preposterous in view of the growing popularity of the field, the large number of trade books so labeled since the war, and the plethora of specialist magazines; nevertheless it is literally true. For every person now writing speculative fiction today there are a dozen writing historical fiction and at least fifty writing contemporary-scene fiction of one sort and another. The editors in any other field have an enormously greater mass of wordage to choose from. I believe that I know, personally or through his work, every regular writer of speculative fiction in the United States today. There are less than a hundred of us all told, both those of us who work at it full time and those of us who give it only part time. There are less than ten of us who make our livings through full-time, free-lance writing of speculative fiction—"ten" is probably too high; I can think of only six by name—and I am sure that I know all the full-timers.

With such a corporal's guard to draw from, how can we be expected to turn out very many great works of literature? We can't and we don't.

As a result of the excess of demand over supply a great many poor speculative novels have reached hard covers these past few years. Anything readable and even moderately entertaining could be sure of publication—it has been a classic case of "We don't want it good; we want it Wednesday."

This great demand has frequently resulted in authors with well-established literary reputations in other fields attempting to turn an easy dollar by whipping off a "science fiction" story or two. In most cases they have fallen flat on their scholarly faces, for this is not an art to be practiced successfully without hard and prayerful preparation. No man in his right mind would attempt a novel concerning the era of the Emperor Justinian without tedious research; the corollary is still more emphatically true when the "main stream" writer tackles speculative fiction. He simply can't do it, despite finished narrative technique, unless he already has, or painfully acquires, the necessary special knowledge.

Unfortunately, for these reasons, I do not think that we are likely to have a large volume of competent, literate speculative fiction in the foreseeable future. Those of you who are addicted to it in quantity must perforce resign yourselves to reading much that is second rate. The situation can be expected to improve slowly as demand eventually results in a larger number of competent writers in this field—but only slowly.

There is not space to discuss in detail the competent, literate speculative fiction which has been written, but I will give a list of speculative novels which I consider to be competent, and of literary merit by any standards. It is not a definitive list and represents simply a sample of my own taste, but these are examples of what I mean by good works in this field: *General Manpower*, by John S. Martin; *Not This August* and *Takeoff*, both by Cyril M. Kornbluth; *Man's Mortality*, by Michael Arlen; *Woman Alive*, by Susan Ertz; *It Can't Happen Here*, by Sinclair Lewis; *1984*, by George Orwell; *The War With the Newts*, by Karel Capek; *Pebble in the Sky* and *The Caves of Steel*, both by Isaac Asimov; *Needle*, by Hal Clement; *Nerves*, by Lester del Rey; *Seven Famous Novels*, by H. G. Wells; *To Walk the Night*, by William Sloane; *Odd*

John, by Olaf Stapledon; *The Doomsday Men*, by J. B. Priestley; *Brave New World*, by Aldous Huxley; *Lest Darkness Fall*, by L. Sprague de Camp; *I Am Thinking of My Darling*, by Vincent McHugh; *The World Below*, by S. Fowler Wright, and *Prelude to Space*, by Arthur C. Clarke.

For comparison, let me list a few fantasies, good by any criteria: *The Sword in the Stone*, by T. H. White; *Alice in Wonderland*, by Lewis Carroll (Charles L. Dodgson); *The Wind in the Willows*, by Kenneth Grahame; *The Wizard of Oz*, by L. Frank Baum; *Out of the Silent Planet*, by C. S. Lewis and the collections *Thirteen O'Clock*, by Stephen Vincent Benét, and *Fancies and Goodnights*, by John Collier.

Again for comparison, two good contemporary-scene novels, in my opinion, are Herman Wouk's *The Caine Mutiny* and Pat Frank's *Hold Back the Night*, and examples of good historical novels by contemporary authors are Paul Wellman's *The Female* and MacKinlay Kantor's *Long Remember*. I think that science fiction, to be worthy of critical literary praise, should approximate the standards of these four novels and of the fantasies mentioned just above.

I had hoped to discuss the history of science fiction. However, there is in print one comprehensive history covering the field from the distant past to about 1935: J. O. Bailey's *Pilgrims Through Space and Time*. This is Dr. Bailey's dissertation for his Ph.D. and it is amazing to me that any university accepted the subject in view of the low esteem in which speculative fiction is held in most departments of English.

Of what use is science fiction? I have already said that it is not prophecy, that most of it is not very good from a literary standpoint . . . and now let me add that much of it is not even very entertaining in my opinion. Good heavens! Does it have any virtue?

Yes. It is the most alive, the most important, the most useful, and the most comprehensive fiction being published today. It is the only fictional medium capable of interpreting the changing, head-long rush of modern life. Speculative fiction is the main stream of fiction—not, as most critics assume, the historical novel and the contemporary-scene novel. On behalf of all my science fiction colleagues I have no intention of being modest about this. The speculative novel is both more important and more difficult than the so-called main-stream novel. Speculative fiction has been expected to stand, hat in hand, a barely recognized illegitimate cousin of the "respectable" forms of literature. I claim for speculative fiction the prior place, the head of the table, even if I have to step on some tender feelings to seat it there.

The historical novel will always have an important place in literature and I have no criticism to make of historical fiction now being written save to note that plunging necklines and bedroom scenes are not in themselves a substitute for honest research. On the other hand the conscientious and competent historical novelist (of whom there are many) is assisted in creating a true picture of times past by the recent increase in freedom to describe in frank terms customs differing from ours.

But historical fiction can never be as useful to the human race as speculative fiction can be (and sometimes is) for the very reason that historical fiction concerns the past. The past can be instructive and very interesting—but the future is far more important . . . to us, to our children, to our children's children. We cannot drive safely by looking only in the rear-view mirror; it is more urgent to watch the road ahead. Too much emphasis on historical fiction partakes of the attitude of the fabulous bird who flew backwards because he didn't care where he was going but liked to see where he had been. Nevertheless, historical fiction has its proper and useful place.

But as for contemporary-scene literature, it is sick with a deep sickness—in its present state it cannot possibly interpret this fast-changing world. Time was when the novel of contemporary life could satisfy most reasonable needs of the spirit, back in a quieter, less rapidly changing day, back when the advancing front of human knowledge was not turning the whole world topsy-turvy every few years. But those quiet days are gone, not to return in your lifetime nor mine, nor in the predictable future. Most novels of contemporary life today tragically fail to live up to the needs of our times.

I am not speaking now of the detective story, the adventure story, or any other genre intended solely as entertainment. Nor am I condemning every novel offered as a serious interpretation of the contemporary scene—there are a number of fine ones. But I am condemning the overwhelming majority.

A very large part of what is accepted as "serious" literature today represents nothing more than a cultural lag on the part of many authors, editors and critics—a retreat to the womb in the face of a world too complicated and too frightening for their immature spirits. A sick literature. What do we find so often today? Autobiographical novels centered around neurotics, even around sex maniacs, concerning the degraded, the psychotic, or the "po' white trash" of back-country farms portrayed as morons or worse, novels about the advertising industry or some other equally narrow area of human experience such as the personal life of a television idol or the experiences of a Park Avenue call girl.

Ah, but this is "realism"! Some of it is, some of it decidedly is not. In any case, is it not odd that the ash-can school of realism, as exemplified by Henry Miller, Jean-Paul Sartre, James Joyce, Françoise Sagan and Alberto Moravia, should be held up to us as "high art" at the very time when all other forms of art are striving to achieve more significant and more interesting forms of expression? Can James Joyce and Henry Miller and their literary sons and grandsons interpret the seething new world of atomic power and antibiotics and interplanetary travel? I say not. In my opinion a very large portion of what is now being offered the public as serious, contemporary-scene fiction is stuff that should not be printed, but told only privately—on a psychiatrist's couch. The world, the human race, is now faced with very real and pressing problems. They will not be solved by introverted neurotics intent on telling, in a tedious hundred thousand words, they hate their fathers and love their mothers.

In any case, I, for one, am heartily sick of stories about frustrates, jerks, homosexuals and commuters who are unhappy with their wives—for goodness sake! Let them find other wives, other jobs—and shut up!

True, some of this sick literature does shine some light into dark corners of the human soul. Even a sordid, narrow novel such as James Jones' *From Here to Eternity* can sometimes manage that. But is this enough? Does it meet the challenge of our century? At best such a novel shows only one frame of a complex and rapidly moving picture.

"I am a stranger and afraid in a world I never made."

Not true! "I am not a stranger and I am not afraid in a world I am helping to make . . . and I am 'damned from here to eternity' only if I abandon my human intelligence and, sheeplike, give up the struggle!"—that is the answer of science fiction, that is why it is alive when most of our current literature is sick and dying. Change . . . change . . . endless change—that is the keynote of our times, whether we face it or run away from it. The mature speculative novel is the only form of fiction which stands even a chance of interpreting the spirit of our times. Most literature has cut itself out of the competition by refusing to deal with the all-too-evident facts—most writers in other fields could not deal properly with the world today even if they tried; their education is too limited, their private world too narrow. They wear blinders.

Speculative fiction is the only form of fiction which does not exclude any area of human experience . . . and in particular it does not exclude that most truly human of all human activities, the one that sets us above animals: the exercise of the scientific method and the sober consideration of the consequences thereof. This is an era when the scientific method, its meaning and use, is indispensable to the mature man— we either use it, or we and our free democratic culture will go under. And yet most modern novelists find no need for it, are even afraid of it. True, they reflect a sickness in the culture, not alone a sickness in themselves. I refer to the increasingly strong trend toward anti-intellectualism, anti-science, demands for a "moratorium" in science, screwball cults and philosophies such as Zen Buddhism (Gautama Buddha must be spinning in his grave!), existentialism, astrology —I once counted more than a dozen different astrology magazines on a newsstand which had not one magazine on astronomy and only one on science in general.

But it is so much easier to consult the stars! So it is. It makes life simple to blame failures on a horoscope. It is much harder to study ballistics, study engineering, try to reach those stars—but it is a much more mature activity. It is always hard to face up to a complex world, try to figure out what makes it tick, try to cope with it, survive and triumph over it.

But this is precisely what science fiction strives toward . . . and what most so-called "main-stream" literature does not even attempt. It used to be that mature men discussed the world and its meaning through the speculative essay. The speculative essay is almost extinct today; it is rarely written, still more rarely published. Its place has been taken by speculative fiction, a tool which, properly handled, is more subtle and more versatile than is the speculative essay. By means of science fiction one can (as one does in mathematics) examine the extremes of a social problem, search it for inflexures, feel out its changing slopes. Nearly all stories in the "mainstream," by their very frameworks, are forever self-excluded from this important form of analysis. Through science fiction the human race can try experiments in imagination too critically dangerous to try in fact. Through such speculative experiments science fiction can warn against dangerous solutions, urge toward better solutions. Science fiction joyously tackles the real and pressing problems of our race, wrestles with them, never ignores them—problems which other forms of fiction cannot challenge. For this reason I assert that science fiction is the most realistic, the most serious, the most significant, the most sane and healthy and human fiction being published today.

I must add that some interlopers have sneaked in under the back of the tent and are masquerading as science fiction. I refer to the "anti-science fiction" which sometimes appears labeled as science fiction, both in books and magazines. This stuff is still another symptom of the neurotic, sometimes pathologic, anti-intellectualism all too common today; it is the wail of the grown-up infant unwilling and perhaps unable to bring reason and reasoned action to bear on our pressing problems. Instead it offers a "devil theory" in which "science" is something outside of and inimical to the human race and "scientists" the inhuman high priests thereof. It reminds me of a plaint attributed (perhaps unjustly) to one United States Senator: "Why in the world were those scientists ever trusted with the secret of the A-bomb in the first place?"

I cannot sympathize with this hatred of science. Scientists are human beings, not devils, and they are engaged in that most typically human of all human activities, the attempt to understand the laws of nature. I myself am satisfied with the laws of nature as they are and I think it is virtuous to try to understand them. I do not believe that the Lord God Almighty made a stupid error when He created uranium.

But you will recognize anti-science fiction when you see it. Its childish, screaming, afraid-of-the-dark hysteria is easy to spot.

I claim one positive triumph for science fiction, totally beyond the scope of so-called main-stream fiction. It has prepared the youth of our time for the coming age of space. Interplanetary travel is no shock to youngsters, no matter how unsettling it may be to calcified adults. Our children have been playing at being space cadets and at controlling rocket ships for quite some time now. Where did they get this healthy orientation? From science fiction and nowhere else. Science fiction can perform similar service to the race in many other fields. For the survival and health of the human race one crudely written science fiction story containing a single worthwhile new idea is more valuable than a bookcaseful of beautifully written non-science fiction.

In a broader sense, all science fiction prepares young people to live and survive in a world of ever-continuing change by teaching them early that the world does change. Since that is the only sort of world we have, science fiction leads in the direction of mental health, of adaptability. In a more specific sense, science fiction preaches the need for freedom of the mind and the desirability of knowledge; it teaches that prizes go to those who study, who learn, who soak up the difficult fields of knowledge such as mathematics and engineering and biology. And so they do! The prizes of this universe go only to those able and equipped to reach out for them. In short, science fiction is preparing our youngsters to be mature citizens of the galaxy . . . as indeed they will have to be.

Where does science fiction go from here?—remembering that much of it is crude and not too competent. We can expect it slowly to increase in amount and quality. We should not expect it ever to become mass entertainment, as it is directed primarily at the superior young person and secondarily at his thoughtful elder. But serious and mature literature has never been mass entertainment; most fiction in all fields in all ages has been trivial and even trashy. Most people read classics of literature only under classroom compulsion and never touch them again. I see no reason to think that this will change in the foreseeable future and certainly no reason why the growth of a mature science fiction should be expected to change it.

I do expect to see some decrease in the neurotic and psychotic fiction now being palmed off on us as "serious literature"; I expect, perhaps too optimistically, that both editors and critics will someday begin to catch up with the real world and quit nursing such nonsense.

In the meantime, to that extent to which science fiction influences its readers toward greater knowledge, more independence of thought, and wider intellectual horizons, it serves its prime function.

While I alone am accountable for the opinions and assertations contained in this discussion, I would be remiss were I not to say that my thoughts have been strongly influenced by others. Among these others are Willy Ley, Reginald Bretnor, Dr. E. E. Smith, Dr. E. T. Bell, Arthur C. Clarke, John W. Campbell, Jr., William A. P. White, G. Harry Stine, Damon Knight, L. Sprague de Camp and Dr. Isaac Asimov. In particular, anyone who has had the pleasure of reading Mr. Bretnor's critical writings will see at once the extent of my indebtedness to him. The above is an incomplete list of the living; I could not list the dead, but among them are T. H. Huxley (*Essays*), Socrates (*Apologia*), and A. Korzybski (*Science and Sanity*).

The references cited below are also incomplete:

The Checklist of Fantastic Literature, edited by Everett F. Bleiler, Shasta Publishers, 1948.

In Search of Wonder—essays on modern science fiction, by Damon Knight, Advent:Publishers, 1956.

Modern Science Fiction: Its Meaning and Its Future, symposium edited by Reginald Bretnor, Coward-McCann, 1953.

Pilgrims Through Space and Time, by J. O. Bailey, Argus Books, 1947.

Index to the Science Fiction Magazines, 1926-1950, by Don Day, Perri Press, 1952.

"On Taking Science Fiction Seriously," by Reginald Bretnor, *The Science Fiction Advertiser*, Vol. VII, No. 1, Winter, 1953-54.

C. M. KORNBLUTH

the failure of the science fiction novel as social criticism

M Y TOPIC IS THE SCIENCE FICTION NOVEL AS Social Criticism. I might be happier discussing the Science Fiction Novel as Fun for One and All, or the Science Fiction Novel as Psychotherapy for the Neurotic Author, but there is a job to be done and I am willing to do my best with it. In doing this job I've tried to use the methods of modern literary criticism, so what follows may sometimes sound wild, impudent and vulgar. This is because modern literary criticism sometimes is wild, impudent and vulgar; anybody who wants to keep

* Based on a lecture delivered January 11, 1957, University College, The University of Chicago.

his dignity had better avoid criticism and stick to scholarship. I should also warn you that I'm going to make a lot of mistakes, and I say this not as a display of becoming modesty but as a prediction, I've gone out on a number of limbs, deliberately, because my intention is to stimulate discussion rather than to terminate it.

Out on Limb Number One, I suggest that the science fiction novel is not an important medium of social criticism. Let us look at some novels of social criticism which did things, and ask ourselves whether any science fiction novel ever remotely matched their records of performance.

Imprimis, *Don Quixote*: a mundane tale about a lunatic, a fat little man, innkeepers and other real people wandering through a real, contemporary Spanish landscape. The professors tell us it blasted away the pretensions of chivalry in one great gale of laughter, ending an ancient social system and way of thought.

Item, *Uncle Tom's Cabin*: another mundane, contemporary story about real people in a contemporary situation. Whether or not Mr. Lincoln said to Harriet Beecher Stowe, "So you are the little lady who started this great war," nobody denies that her book played a part in history.

Item, *The Jungle*, by Upton Sinclair. I'm afraid I can't avoid repeating Sinclair's rueful comment, "I aimed at the nation's heart and hit its stomach." This is perfectly true, and he hit hard. His mundane, contemporary novel about immigrant life in Chicago directly caused a sweeping revision of American law and practice in the processing of meat. God knows how many lives, and how many millions of man-hours of illness, have been saved by this book.

Item, *The Good Soldier Schweik*, by Jaroslav Hasek. This contemporary novel about a most uncommon common soldier in the Austro-Hungarian Imperial Army is supposed to have helped to bring down the Austro-Hungarian Empire, playing the same sort of role as *Uncle Tom's Cabin*.

Item, *Babbitt*, by Sinclair Lewis. Lewis showed middle-class America the tragic emptiness of its life without culture, and lived to see that middle-class life strikingly transformed. I don't pretend that you and I live in a golden age of culture, but we do have everywhere today our readers of books, our listeners to music, our thinkers and appreciators where before we had—Babbitts.

Another great book stands somewhere outside the canon: *Gargantua and Pantagruel*, by François Rabelais. Drastic social criticism it certainly is, but I do not know whether anybody claims it ever converted a single soul from Calvinism or monastic dourness to delight in the senses and the intellect. I do know that there are idiots at large who are capable of arguing that the book is a science fiction novel; if anybody tries to embroil me in such an argument I will punch him in the nose.

There is a curious fact about five of the six books I've mentioned. Each has added a word to the permanent international vocabulary: "quixotic," "Simon Legree," "schweikism" (heard more often in Europe than here, but not quite unknown in America) "babbittry" and "gargantuan" (mostly misused). This little touchstone is by no means a bad test of the influence of a book. Living words like "odyssey," "scrooge" and "romeo" are living witnesses to the power of literary works they derived from.

Some of the amateur scholars of science fiction are veritable Hitlers for aggrandizing their field. If they perceive in, say, a sixteenth century satire some vaguely speculative element they see it as a trembling and persecuted minority, demand *Anschluss*, and proceed to annex the satire to science fiction. This kind of empire-building has resulted in an impressive list of titles allegedly science-fictional going back to classic times or for all I know earlier. Assume they are all veritable science fiction. Most of these works are of no importance. Not one of them has been influential to a degree remotely comparable with the mundane books I've cited so far. The books I've cited have measurably done things; there is general agreement by sane men that they started wars, they caused revolutions, they got laws passed, they changed customs and attitudes. No science fiction novel has done anything like this, even though science fiction contains a high percentage of explicit and implicit social criticism. After a digression I will climb out on Limb Number Two and tell you why I think this is so.

The digression is into a chapter from Melville's *Moby Dick*. It is Chapter XL, called "Midnight, Forecastle." Ahab is not present, Ishmael takes no part, Moby Dick is not mentioned and the mates are no more than offstage voices. For six pages some sailors lounge about off watch, sing a little, dance a little and talk. There is a near-fight between two of them, but it is broken up when a mate calls for all hands to reef sail; a squall has blown up. The chapter ends.

From this description it would seem that Melville's ostensible purpose was to add to the reality of the *Pequod*, to fill corners of the picture with corroborative detail, to further the suspension of disbelief. But an attentive reading reveals something more. A Dutch sailor speaks: "Grand snoozing tonight, maty; fat night for that. I mark this in our old Mogul's wine . . ." A subtle onomatopoeia pervades the speech; note the predominance of long, drawling vowels and diphthongs and open-ended consonants. Then a French sailor speaks: "Hist, boys! Let's have a jig or two before we ride to anchor in Blanket Bay. What say ye? There comes the other watch. Stand by all legs! Pip! little Pip!" The vowels are mostly short, most of the consonants are stopped; the effect is of a string of firecrackers; the contrast with the speech of the Dutch sailor is as strong as it can be.

At this point we can be sure that Melville is up to something, that this dialogue is not mere stenography. He is showing us two types of mankind; why? The effect becomes stranger as we read on; Pip complains that a jingler has dropped off his tambourine, and a Chinese sailor calls to him: "Rattle thy teeth, then, and pound away; make a pagoda of thyself." This is not naturalistic speech and we must by now admit that a new quality has crept into the passage. A stenographic, naturalistic explanation no longer suffices. This new quality is considered desirable by modern criticism. It has been called ambiguity, multiordinality, plurisignation and symbolism. I shall call it symbolism. Now, once we admit the presence of the symbolic quality in Chapter XL we must admit that Melville's characters are acting out the ostensible melodrama against the backdrop of the forecastle, but that another higher drama is being performed simultaneously by whatever it is they symbolize.

Continuing to read, we find that this sailor then turns his thoughts to women—the Tahitian sailor to the "holy nakedness of our dancing girls"; the Sicilian sailor complaining "Tell me not of it!" and then going on to invoke "fleet interlacings of the limbs—lithe swayings—coyings—flutterings! lip! heart! hip! all graze . . ." Most pathetic of all is the reverie of the nameless Manx sailor who it seems never knew any woman but prostitutes and is now too old for them; but who nevertheless misses their company; for they come obsessively into his mind. He watches the sailors dancing to Pip's tambourine and says to himself: "I wonder whether these jolly lads bethink them of what they are dancing over. I'll dance over your grave, I will—that's the bitterest threat of your night-women, that beat head-winds round corners. O Christ! to think of the green navies and the green-skulled crews! Well, well; belike the whole world's a ball, as you scholars have it; and so 'tis right to make one ball-room of it. Dance on, lads, you're young; I was once."

I think we know by now whom the sailors symbolize. They represent every soldier, sailor and wanderer who was ever far from home and its comforts; they are everybody who ever feared and suffered the great basic experiences of privation, impotence and mortality.

At a great price bought Melville this freedom. He attained symbolic quality in this passage by very hard writing and self-discipline. If he had not carefully built up to it, the wild and improbable cry of the Chinese sailor would evoke only a laugh instead of the eerie feeling, "all this is doubly meaningful." Every writer of contemporary or historical fiction must tame his imagination and think almost as the world thinks, or he is lost. Nobody will take seriously a writer who asserts that Michigan Boulevard is in New York City, or that the second president of the United States was Julius Caesar.

But the science fiction writer is born free. More than any other writer (except the writers of fantasy and dreams) he "makes it all up out of his own head." There is, for instance, no street map now in existence of Fort Worth, Texas, for the year 1995. The person writing about Fort Worth of 1995 is thus perfectly free to make its streets 250 feet wide. Let us say that, in the absence of a Bureau of Vital Statistics report for Fort Worth as of 1995, he populates the city with adults nine feet tall. Nobody will stop him, nobody can stop him, and he may even be paid for doing it. The question is, why should he? What are these nine-foot-tall Texans striding along streets 250 feet wide? What's the good of them? The answer is, of course, that they are ambiguities, multiordinalities, plurisignations, symbols. They are symbols of 1958 Texans, achieved at the stroke of a pen, without hard writing. The science fiction writer churns out symbols every time he writes of the future or an alternate present; he rolls out symbols of people, places, things, relationships, as fast as he can work his typewriter or drive his pen.

What's the good of it? It makes us think. The nine-foot-tall Texans of 1995, ostensibly, make us think of the Texans of 1958 and their customs and values. A symbol makes us think about the thing which it symbolizes. If I felt like adding to the confusion of the terminology I would call a symbol an "idol," for the functions of the symbol and the idol are the same.

Science fiction then should be an effective literature of social criticism—but I have said that it is not. I will climb onto Limb Number Two in an attempt to explain why it is not. I believe that in science fiction the symbolism lies too deep for action to result, that the science fiction story does not turn the reader outward to action but inward to contemplation. I think the unwitting compact between the writer and reader of science fiction goes: "We are suspending reality, you and I. By the signs of the rocket ship and the ray gun and the time machine we indicate that the relationship between us has nothing to do with the real world. By writing the stuff and by reading it we abdicate from action, we give free play to our unconscious drives and symbols, we write and read not about the real world but about ourselves and the things within ourselves."

Bearing in mind this hypothesis that the relationship between science fiction writer and reader is deeper than we had previously supposed, I will survey some science fiction novels containing explicit and implicit social criticism.

The earliest English science fiction novel which is still part of the living literature contains a high concentration of explicit social criticism. I am speaking of *Gulliver's Travels*. You will find it almost invariably is one of the volumes of those mail-order sets of classics, and it must be one of the volumes which do not let the average reader down. *Gulliver* reads well and easily to this day. It's a very funny book, full of good jokes and scatology, and its dominant attitude is the over-popular thesis that people are no damn good.

It has another puzzling asset which seems to have guaranteed its immortality. The image of giant Gulliver among the Lilliputians, and especially the image of Gulliver bound by the little people, strikes a chord in most readers. Perhaps many people cherish an unconscious image of themselves as giants chained by pygmies, and Gulliver Bound evokes this image. Perhaps the symbolism is double, and there is identification with the pygmies as well, with the pygmies symbolizing one's childhood and/or feelings of inferiority. Gulliver Bound is, at any rate, the trademark of the book. No illustrated edition of it omits a picture of this scene, the comic-book versions make great play of it, and it was emphasized both in the American cartoon movie and the Russian puppet movie versions.

Gulliver's Lilliput is a queerly inconsistent place. It is Utopia and Anti-Utopia in the same realm. The court of Lilliput is a scathing parody of the English court in the minutest detail. At the English court, did the courtiers bow, scrape and intrigue to gain membership in three knightly orders whose symbols were bands colored red, blue and green? Very well; in the court of Lilliput the courtiers for hours on end jumped over or crawled under a stick held by the king. Their rewards were silk threads colored blue, red or green—these are symbols of symbols! And pejorative symbolic action may reach an all-time high-water mark in the closing paragraphs of Chapter Five of the Voyage to Lilliput. Therein, Gulliver ostensibly extinguishes a fire in the royal palace by urinating on it. The proof that this is actually a symbolic statement of his opinion of the English court lies in the horror and revulsion with which his ostensibly prudent, good-hearted action is received by the empress.

The inconsistency I referred to is this: the schools of Lilliput are everything Swift thought schools should be and, in England, were not. Bad court, good schools. I will label this a flaw and move on.

There are a great many coined words in the book, and Damon Knight has recently applied to science fiction Kenneth Burke's doctrine that through an author's coined words and puns a critic can gain clues to his conscious and unconscious attitudes and intentions. I have tried this method of inquiry on the Travels with no success. The Lilliputian rank of admiral is galbet, which suggests a portmanteau of gallows and gibbet, which is not especially elucidating. An exception being the name of the flying island: Laputa. Which is simply Spanish for "the whore" as Swift well knew; indeed he devoted a dead-pan half page of fake etymology to supplying an alternate meaning of the word. I suspect that Swift may have coined his words out of tags of Hebrew, Greek and other languages I don't know. The Lilliputian speech, for instance, gives a weird impression of oscillating between Hebrew and Japanese.

The voyage to the flying island of Laputa is of special interest, for it is the closest of the voyages to modern science fiction. Laputa is gadgety and populated by scientists. It criticizes by extrapolation a social trend toward wild-eyed "projects." It contains Swift's celebrated and astonishingly accurate guess at the existence and location of the two satellites of Mars, which were invisible to the telescopes of his day. There is another interesting guess embodied in the few phrases describing the language of the Laputans. Their speech is said to be mathematical, and to an extent musical. "Mathematical speech" is, I think, defensible as a stab at Boolean algebra—maybe as much of a stab as the young Leibnitz' *characteristica universalis*. In each case the speculator said approximately as follows: "Perhaps language and thought can be put on a mathematical basis." And then in 1854 Professor George Boole did exactly that, with earthshaking consequences that will not be fully appreciated in your lifetime or mine.

Typically, Swift disapproved of this mathematical speech. The Voyage to Laputa is not merely science fiction; it belongs to the sub-category of anti-science science fiction. Swift pours his contempt on the scientists of the flying island for neglecting practical affairs, for being all thumbs away from their drafting boards, and ignorant of anything outside their specialties.

In summary, does *Gulliver's Travels* have much more than the interest of a peep-show, or an overheard family quarrel? Does it contain elements of beauty, awe or tragedy? It does not. The meanness of Swift and his time is announced on the first page, where in less than one sentence he describes Gulliver's courtship and marriage as follows: ". . . being advised to alter my condition, I married Miss Mary Burton, second daughter to Mr. Edmund Burton, hosier, in Newgate Street, with whom I received four hundred pounds for a portion."

What is Swift's answer to the great problems of mankind? It is that they should return to primitive virtue, symbolized by horses—the Houyhnhnms. This is the cheap and erroneous doctrine of the noble savage which we get also from Rousseau and which can be disproved by examining any aboriginal culture at all. It is curious that Swift's symbol for primitive virtue should be the horse, and I would like to suggest that there may be an element of atonement in his choice. We have pretty much forgotten that our not very remote ancestors practiced cruelties on animals which would be unthinkable today. Children amused themselves by torturing animals because they were taught they had no feelings. Horses were tamed and trained by savage abuse. There must have been exceptions, but not until 1853 did the English cavalryman Lewis Nolan, and in 1858 the American farmer John S. Rarey, widely publish systems of horse-training by kindness and rewards. The world was ready for Nolan's and Rarey's systems, and horsewhips formerly used for training the animals were thriftily set aside for use on editors or those who spoke lightly of one's sister's virtue. Perhaps Swift glorified the horse in an attempt to make up for the countless cases of whipping, starving and overloading he must have witnessed.

Gulliver's Travels was a rousing, emphatic "success." Did it accomplish anything? No. Perhaps it raised a few titters at the absurdity of English court life or the thoroughly misunderstood activities of the Royal Society. This is not an achievement comparable with the achievements of *The Good Soldier Schweik* or *Uncle Tom's Cabin* or *The Jungle*. It did add a word or two to the international vocabulary—"lilliputian" and "yahoo." Mostly it contributed to the unconscious of its millions of readers. It turns its readers inward, not outward.

I shall take up next social criticism in the science fiction novels of Dr. E. E. Smith. I chose his work deliberately because it represents a major area of science fiction, the large-scale interplanetary story. He was one of the earliest writers to work that vein and one of the most successful. Most science fiction readers know and enjoy his books. They are, in a word, important—too important to ignore.

The early Smith books, the "Skylark" stories, present us, in the realm of social criticism, with a strange blend of naive Marxism, a fascistic leader-principle, and despair of democracy. All this is implicit in the books, of course; I do not for a moment suggest that Dr. Smith was on a soap-box voicing a reasoned-out creed. Nevertheless he wrote what he wrote, and it's legitimate to examine it.

In the "Skylark" books the Earth was rapidly coming under the sway of a vast and villainous steel corporation—ultimately, a Marxist concept. Sympathetically-portrayed alien cultures were shown to be under rigid military discipline analogous to the Spartan. One democratic planet could be so because the intelligence of its inhabitants was enormously advanced beyond the Earthly standard—a pessimistic negative reply is implicit here to the question of whether mankind is capable of self-government.

Some might think it would be best to dismiss these attitudes as mere plot devices, notions that were floating around during the Depression which Dr. Smith hadn't really chewed before swallowing, techniques which had not yet been revealed to the world in their pragmatic fullness as practiced in Germany, Italy and Russia. A steady, clear-eyed look at ancient Sparta would have revealed it as a ghastly tyranny incomplete and unworkable without its murder gangs who marked down for death any peasant showing a spark of initiative or leadership; but scientists and engineers used to be notorious for their lack of broad culture, a situation which now seems to be rapidly changing. We might say that people just weren't interested in democracy in those days before it was threatened, that they accepted it as they accepted the air they breathed. We might compare the "Skylark" attitudes with the supremely fuzzy contemporary statement of H. P. Lovecraft on one of his fictional pre-human races: "Their government was a kind of socialistic fascism."

All this, no doubt, is perfectly true. The fact of its truth however does not rule out the possibility that another explanation is also true. Besides the economic and cultural reasons for the lack of interest in these vital problems of mankind, there may be a psychological reason.

In our search for light, let us as before examine the symbols. Dr. Richard Seaton did not really exist and his voyages did not really happen; the words about them are therefore not a naturalistic report of a real event. What then are the words about? What does Seaton symbolize?

Let us find out what love means in the world of Richard Seaton. It is non-sexual, we find; a mild cuddling is as far as Seaton goes with his wife. They do not have children; children are had by elderly creatures who give the impression of being perpetually in formal evening dress. Dorothy Seaton is a girl, and therefore debarred from any share in the world's real work. Dorothy Seaton is equipped with a doctorate in music and a Stradivarius which, if memory serves, her daddy gave her. However, she plays schmaltzy, *alt Wien* tearoom

numbers which no Doctor of Music ever hooded in the real
world could conceivably perform.

I suggest from this that there is very little fundamental
material in the "Skylark" universe which is congruent with
adulthood. I suggest that there is much fundamental material
in that universe congruent with the attitudes and emotions
of a boy seven or nine years old tearing off down an alley
on his bike in search of adventure. The politics of this boy
are vague, half-understood, overheard adult dogmatisms. His
sex-life is a bashful, inhibited yearning for unspecific contact.
His cultural level is low; he has not had time to learn to like
anything seriously musical. Around the corner there lurks
the impossibly malignant black-haired bully who may be all
of twelve, and his smart little toady. But Dicky Seaton has a
loyal pal, Marty Crane, and together they will whip the bully
and toady in a fair, stand-up fight.

What are these wild adventures of Seaton and Crane, then?
These mighty conquests, these vast explorations, these titanic
battles? They are boyish daydreams, the power fantasies
which compensate for the inevitable frustrations of childhood in an adult world. They are the weakness of the Smith
stories as rational pictures of the universe and society, and
they are the strength of the stories as engrossing tales of
Never-Never Land. We have all been children.

Armed with this concept of the Smith hero as a child,
I turned eagerly to the study of his later series, the "Galactic
Patrol" books. I was curious to learn whether the Smith hero
has grown up or not.

Many things in the "Galactic Patrol" universe are more
adult than their equivalents in the "Skylark" universe.
Womankind has been admitted to the human race. Pro-
creation occurs as a consequence of love. A brilliant gallery
of sympathetically-presented extra-terrestrials atones in full
for the old "Skylark" doctrine that the less human an entity
looks, the more likely it is to be villainous. But all this is

misleading; Seaton and Crane have not grown up. They have grown back.

They have become incredibly powerful because they were good and someone rewarded them with a magic amulet. Social criticism? Well, there is a great deal of crime and vice in their world, but no human being is responsible for it. The crime and vice, the "badness," are successfully combatted in the end, but human beings are not responsible for that either. There are dirty politics and clean politics—but human beings are not responsible for them.

Well then, for what are human beings responsible? They are responsible for propitiating their wise protectors who give them magic amulets; they are responsible for avoiding their terrible and omnipotent assailants. All other activity is meaningless, a mask, a system of levers leading to the only great source of good and evil.

Human beings are, in short, about eighteen months old.

I will leave it up to you to conclude what the slimy, amorphous, evil-smelling ultimate villains of the Lensmen universe symbolize, pointing out only that their name "Eich" is identical with a cry of disgust which might be uttered by the mother of an infant under certain circumstances.

Symbolic regression to infancy, by the way, is not at all unusual in science fiction, and neither is it the end of the line. Dr. Smith's characters have a penchant for climbing into spherical space ships or pear-shaped space ships. His heroic wearers of the Galactic Patrol lens at one time had their headquarters inside an armor-plated hill where they were safe from everything.

Let us contrast the Smith novels with Wilson Tucker's *The Long Loud Silence*. This is an alleged science fiction novel of social criticism in that it is a violent tract against biological warfare. It is the type of novel which says: "I will show you what will happen if you don't listen to me and do as I say." It does not have thick symbolic content; its land is our land, its people are us, transposed only a few years and one insane decision into the future. The book concludes with the stark, enormous deed of cannibalism. This takes us back to the animal, before the human being became human enough to define the first and basic crimes—cannibalism general, within the family incest and unregulated parricide. If these three acts, common in the animal world, had not been prohibited, the family, group life and ultimately civilization would have been impossible. The prohibitions seem to be fairly recent as the life-span of the human race goes; the Greek tragedies were largely concerned with the terrible consequences of parricide and incest even when committed unwittingly; the badness of unwitting cannibalism within the family recurs through the Elizabethan drama, and to our own day in a novel by Evelyn Waugh.

Tremendous power is latent in these symbols, and Tucker brilliantly taps it in the scene of his book. He shows us creatures reduced to eating human flesh and therefore non-human; it is all the more horrible that they are capable of speech and reason.

I will cast aside a part-time principle that biographical information has no place in literary criticism to examine an interesting alternative to Tucker's published ending. Originally he had his protagonist eat his erstwhile mistress, which is pure familial cannibalism. His editor persuaded him to have the two join forces instead to commit cannibalism on stray human beings who crossed their path. I think the editor was wise. We are left not with the substance but with the shadow. We have the taste of familial cannibalism in our mouths, but if we were fed the actual thing we would vomit it out—that is, reject the reality of the book.

I suspect *The Long Loud Silence* is a book of social criticism which might have had the effect of an *Uncle Tom's Cabin* or Upton Sinclair's *The Jungle*. It has no inherent defect which could have kept it from sweeping the country,

bringing home to citizens and voters the realities of bacterio-
logical warfare, and forcing our leaders to take steps toward
lessening the probability that the book will become true.
It is legitimate to ask why it was ignored by the nation.
It was ignored because publishers think of their books in
rigid categories. Tucker's book fell into the category "science
fiction." Books in the category "science fiction" get no promotion or advertising to speak of, they get misleading jacket
blurbs, and a sale of five thousand copies is considered a
realistic target. The idea is to sell it to the science fiction
readers, clear expenses, make a little money on the paperback
reprint, pat the author on the back and tell him to go write
another book, boy, we love your stuff.

We happy few who have read *The Long Loud Silence* must
agree that it is enormously effective social criticism, saying
much about man and his society. It makes us think; it makes
us want to act. In this it contrasts strongly with the books
of Dr. Smith. I suggest that this is because Tucker's book
is mature where Dr. Smith's books are not. Tucker is writing
about adults in situations analogous to those you and I encounter, real situations, social situations, social problems with
social answers. Dr. Smith is writing about children whose
problems, while they exist, are not social problems. The
problems in the books of Dr. Smith are person-to-person and
one-thing-at-a-time. There is no sense of a social webwork
of relationships and interactions.

Now you may object that I proclaimed from Limb Number
Two that science fiction is too deeply symbolic to evoke
action from the reader, yet here I am saying that only an
accidental habit of the publishing trade kept *The Long Loud
Silence* from evoking action. I am not much of a one for
those interminable arguments about what is and what isn't
science fiction, but this once I'll join in and say that Tucker's
novel, though set a few years in the future, is not science
fiction. Perhaps in my zeal I am setting up a vicious-circle

fallacy here, but I doubt it. Point to the things that mean science fiction and what do we see? Vast spaces, strange inventions, great voyages, heroes incredible, villains satanic, monsters, strangeness. We do not find these things in Tucker's book, and I maintain that he has not written a science fiction novel but a first-rate contemporary novel about a war and its aftermath.

Let us look next at the science fiction books of Olaf Stapledon. In his works I find an obsessive master theme of personalities merging, flowing together, to form something greater than the sum of its parts. In *Odd John* this was the pooled mind of the superchildren, with a physical parallel in their lonely island away from everybody. In *Last and First Men* it was the Martian invaders who could merge physically and mentally, and it was the group mind of the human race in communion. In *Starmaker* it was the group mind of the interstellar travelers and it was also "the supreme moment of the universe." This occurred when every mind in the cosmos merged and through this coalescence managed to achieve what has always been regarded as the supreme good, knowledge of God.

Does anybody think of Stapledon as a social critic? I believe not, and yet he intended to be; he tried to be. He wrote down a detailed indictment of contemporary life in *The Last Men in London*, and nobody reads it. He does it more briefly in part of *Last and First Men*, and Basil Davenport rightly omits this part from his one-volume edition of Stapledon's works. He writes a book called *Waking World* urging sanity on us all, and we will have nothing to do with it. Perhaps he sensed this rejection; the later book *Sirius*, resorting to the ancient method of *The Golden Ass* to examine mankind through the eyes of an intelligent animal, is bitter, almost savage.

There is part of Stapledon which we reject and part which we embrace. We embrace his bigness, his daring to write in billions of years. We embrace his wonderful fertility of invention which fills the planets of his universe with strange but plausible beasts and men. We embrace his piercing, endless quest for meaning. We embrace his obsession with coalescence; that is the stuff religious ceremonies, Nuremberg Party Days, sales pep meetings and family reunions are made of; we all of us at one time or another yearn to flow together. And his social criticism? We sweep it under the carpet. This is easy enough to prove if you move in science fiction fan circles; you have only to ask some fans whether they think of Stapledon as a social critic or not, and they'll say they don't. Fans fairly represent Stapledon's relatively few readers.

We come next to a book which has had many more readers than anything Stapledon wrote, *1984* by George Orwell. I believe the same situation exists with respect to social criticism versus science fiction values in *1984* as in Stapledon's books, that is, that the science fiction values swamped the social criticism. I can imagine a program of depth interviews and opinion polls which might prove my belief, but without a grant from the Ford Foundation I can't go beyond imagining it.

I can prove that Orwell was consciously, deliberately, writing *1984* as propaganda—and I say propaganda without apologies. There is nothing evil about the thing itself, and unless social criticism is also propaganda, it is mere whimpering. Toward the end of his life Orwell knew exactly who he was and what he was doing. His essays tell us that everything he wrote was polemic and political. He did novels and he also did the odd jobs he thought should be done which nobody else was doing. He did critical studies of comic postcards and boys' newspapers in a spirit of deliberately humorless intensity. He wanted to find out what these media had to say about the English working class and what their implications were for his primary tasks of combatting tyranny and establishing socialism. He delved into the structure of the

English language and wrote an essay on how to write about politics without being nonsensical; this to him was also related to combatting tyranny and establishing socialism. We may take it for granted that he wrote *1984* to help combat tyranny and establish socialism.

The second part of his program was little noticed, which was an old story to Orwell; his earlier books, *Animal Farm* specifically, said that the rulers of Russia were no damned good; that the final proof of this was you could hardly tell the Russian rulers from the rulers of Germany and England. Nobody seemed to notice this; they merrily went ahead and used the book as a stick to beat Russia with.

Now, has *1984*, with its enormous circulation, done anything to combat tyranny? Lacking that Ford Foundation grant I mentioned, I can only say that I think it did not. Call me Procrustes and let's move along.

The book is an almost arrogantly good novel. The prose is the prose of a man with an English public school education, and I have noticed that these old Eton and Cambridge boys can write rings around anybody unfortunate enough not to have attended a public school and an ancient university. The book has structure; a beginning, middle and end, balanced and proportionate. It has fully realized characters and, as it "should" be in a novel, these are protagonist, antagonist, heroine, comic relief (that's Parsons) and spear-carriers. It is an added pleasure to read a book that matter-of-factly accepts formal limitations and works within them at high intensity. The reporting could not be improved on; Orwell selects the relevant detail every time, knows the importance of trivia, bangs sense-impressions at us until we see, hear, taste, feel and smell the world of *1984*.

Orwell is the writer in a hundred thousand who notices and remarks that not only the taste but the texture on the tongue of coffee with sugar is different from the texture of coffee with saccharin.

The book is unusual in that it is written on one literal and two symbolic levels, one apparently semi-conscious and the other I think wholly unconscious. On the semi-conscious level *1984* is almost an allegory of growing up in middle-class England. We know from Orwell's long essay "Such, Such Were the Joys" that he did not think his childhood was an easy one, and this could readily be inferred also from *1984*. We have only to think of Winston Smith as a boy and of the inquisitor O'Brien as his father for many things to fall kaleido-scopically into a sudden new design.

Sexual activity is forbidden to Winston Smith as it is to a boy under pain of dire punishment.

There are no laws or clear-cut rules of conduct for Winston Smith to obey; he, like a child, may transgress without meaning to. He must not only do what is right, he must *be good.*

The uncanny O'Brien always knows what Winston Smith is thinking. (When I was a small boy my mother used to privately report my misconduct of the day to my father when he came home; he would then pretend to "read it on my forehead.")

O'Brien is large and powerful; Winston is small and weak.

O'Brien practices incredible brutalities on Winston in the name of "education"; Winston believes this and continues to like O'Brien. At any moment during the torture one expects the inquisitor to say "This hurts me more than it hurts you," but that would have given the game away.

And in one damnably strange passage, O'Brien says to Winston: ". . . is there anything that you wish to say before you leave? Any message? Any question?" At this point Winston's mind should be boiling with a thousand questions about the mysterious Brotherhood he has just joined, but he asks none of them. What he does ask is: "Did you ever happen to hear of an old rhyme that begins *Oranges and lemons, say the bells of St. Clement's?*"

"Again O'Brien nodded. With a sort of grave courtesy he completed the stanza:

" '... *When I grow rich, say the bells of Shoreditch.*' "

Tell me a story, Daddy.

This symbolic level, the level of boyhood, I have described as semi-conscious. The many parallels between Winston Smith as an adult in London and Eric Blair (Orwell's real name) as a schoolboy at "Crossgates" described in "Such, Such Were the Joys" could hardly have escaped the creator of them both. To Winston Smith, O'Brien's "face seen from below looked coarse and worn, with pouches under the eyes and tired lines from nose to chin." This is just how young Eric sees adults, almost word for word. Young Eric confusedly believes that every adult is in league with the school's headmaster and will drop everything to report him if he misbehaves—paralleling the Thought Police and the swarming amateur informers. Young Eric suffered from the school's squalor and lack of privacy, and what Winston Smith desperately wants is just a little cleanliness and a room of his own with no spying telescreen. It is clear that Orwell deliberately drew on recollections of his childhood for *1984*, and we should note that he explicitly equipped Winston Smith with a complicated feeling of guilt about his mother. I sense, however, both in his essay and the novel a failure to come to grips with the relationship between father and son. In the essay his memories of his father are unbelievably meagre—father was just an irritable man who always said "Don't!" Similarly Smith's father is curiously absent from his consciousness.

So far we have cruised the surface of the novel and taken a short submarine tour through its depths. I now invite you to join me in the bathysphere and descend to the ocean floor. Let us consider first a curious architectural feature of *1984* introduced to us in the following passage: "... in the side wall, within easy reach of Winston's arm, (was) a large oblong slit protected by a wire grating. This last was for the disposal of waste paper. Similar slits existed in thousands or tens of thousands throughout the building, not only in every room but at short intervals in every corridor. For some reason they were nicknamed memory holes. When one knew that any document was due for destruction, or even when one saw a scrap of waste paper lying about, it was an automatic action to lift the flap of the nearest memory hole and drop it in, whereupon it would be whirled away on a current of warm air to the enormous furnaces which were somewhere in the recesses of the building."

The same devices can be found in the fictional future of Robert Heinlein. Heinlein, however, by analogy with a term out of mediaeval architecture and because of their function, calls them "oubliettes"—from the French verb oublier, "to forget." This is the sensible thing to call them. Orwell calls them the exact opposite of what they are. Perhaps on one level this harmonizes with the culture of the time—Freedom is Slavery, Ignorance is Strength, War is Peace. Perhaps the name has another level of meaning, which I shall take up shortly.

Before I do, let us look at Room 101, the torture room in the Ministry of Love. I suggest that Room 101 is Orwell's unconscious symbol for the uterus. My reasons are:

Room 101 is obviously the first room in the numbering system; the starting place.

It is a room below ground in the center of a white, windowless pyramid named the Ministry of Love—female symbolism can scarcely go further than that.

The three numerals 101 displayed on a page constitute a naive sketch of the female genitalia seen from below.

"Room" is a pun for "womb," underscored by the two "w" sounds which crowd along after it, as if to correct the "r" sound.

The uterine symbolism of Room 101, by the way, was perceived and exploited in the movie version of *1984*—Winston Smith was delivered into the room by way of a cylindrical passage.

Now let us look at those slits protected by liftable skirts "for some reason . . . nicknamed memory holes." I suggest that the illogical name is an unconscious pun for femaleness. "Memory" is close to "mammary." The first syllable, "mem," is the Anglo-Indian word for "lady," and Orwell was born an Anglo-Indian. And there is a whole cluster of childhood names for mother which are more or less close to "memory"—"mum," "mummy" and so on.

The memory holes and Room 101 have this in common: they symbolize torment and destruction in the womb. The question we must face is, why does the uterus symbolize for Orwell a place of torment where destruction and "the worst thing in the world" happens to everybody? The uterus is supposed to be the place of warmth and safety. I cannot help wondering whether Orwell's birth was a long and painful one, and whether his mother suffered a near miscarriage or two while pregnant with him.

We are now almost outside the area of literary criticism, but not quite. I believe that some readers may find *1984* meaningful and compelling or unreal and revolting on an unconscious basis of agreement or disagreement with Orwell's image of the uterus as a place of torment.

I hope nobody will conclude that I am deprecating Orwell's work or character by discussing it in this fashion. I say this only because some time ago the critic Anthony West of the *New Yorker* wrote on Orwell. To his own satisfaction he traced most of Orwell's themes back to his unhappy school experiences. Unless I misread him, he concluded that because of this Orwell's work and even Orwell's manhood were so much the less. I regard this conclusion as a howling non sequitur. I think Orwell was a great writer and led as useful and noble a life as can be imagined for a twentieth century man.

Now, what about *The Space Merchants*, alias "Gravy Planet," by Frederik Pohl and myself? Apparently it is accepted as an outstanding example in recent science fiction of the department of social criticism called satire. The characteristic quality of satire in symbolic terms seems to be that it offers the reader a great quantity of symbols each of which is rather close to the object symbolized. As I leaf through the book I see that Pohl and I left virtually nothing in American life untransformed, from breakfast food to the Presidency of the United States. I see that with almost lunatic single-mindedness we made everything in our future America that could be touched, tasted, smelled, heard, seen or talked about bear witness to the dishonesty of the concepts and methods of today's advertising.

I don't claim any high literary merit for the book; if I were asked to rewrite it today it would come out a much less plotty job, and Pohl agrees with me on this. But it did have some effect. It stimulated thinking in a lot of places, some of them quite unlikely ones. There was a full-page review, for instance, in *The Industrial Worker*, the organ of such I.W.W. members, or Wobblies, as survive. I have reason to believe it was read by a lot of people who do not normally read science fiction. It had a vogue in the New York City theatrical crowd, an actor has told me, and I know it was read by broadcasting men across the country. It was read, of course, by the hypersensitive advertising people. In their trade paper *Tide* a reviewer wanted to know whether it was supposed to be good, clean fun or the most vicious, underhanded attack on the advertising profession yet. (If he had asked me, I would have told him "Both.") It is not dead yet, either. A radio version has been given and it may one day appear as a musical comedy. It is too soon to write off *The Space Merchants* as just another science fiction book which has shot its wad and been forgotten. Naturally I hope that it will have some real influence on American advertising, and I do state that the probability of this is not, as of today, 0.0000.

Arthur Clarke has complained of science fiction books like *The Space Merchants* that they are too ugly, that they should contain elements of love and beauty counterpoising the elements of ugliness and death. In this, as I have told him, he is perfectly correct. I think the book is flawed at least to that extent. What love there is in the book keeps turning into hate. There is a marked hostility to women throughout. This seems to be an unexpected and unwanted by-product of its collaborative authorship, since hostility to women does not turn up to that degree in my solo work or Pohl's. This essentially unrealistic concentration on the seamy side, I believe, made it impossible for us to bring off our happy ending. By the time the reader has gone through 178 pages of misery, animosity, squalor and violence, he is understandably reluctant to believe that on Page 179 everything can suddenly be patched up so that these savage creatures can live happily ever after.

There is some discussion in science fiction circles at this time about sadism in literature. I think a character in *The Space Merchants* can throw light on the subject. The arguments go as follows: Critic says, stop portraying ugly, meaningless violence in your stories; that is sadism and it breeds sadism. Writer replies: Ugly, meaningless violence is a part of life and I am portraying life.

The character Hedy, the skinny girl with the needle, might be described as a sadist's sadist. She is shown practicing sadism and getting a bang out of it. Yet there have been no complaints that I know of about her. I think this is because she is specifically labelled as a sick, deranged person. In this case the writers have been able to present ugly, meaningless violence and thus round out the reality of their story, and yet nobody seems to feel that sadism is being taught to or urged on the predisposed reader. There is a poison label firmly pasted on the sadistic episode and it seems to have done its job.

I have mostly been discussing until now social criticisms with which I agree. There are also social criticisms with which I do not agree. They are implicit in the "menace" story and its subclass, the "monster" story. If I wanted to make some money in a hurry and didn't care how, I'd write a "monster" story. I am not referring to stories like "Who Goes There?" by John W. Campbell, Jr. That is a story about maintaining integrity, working together, using brains and courage to solve the problems of survival in an indifferent world. I am referring to stories like *The Shrinking Man* by Richard Matheson.

Such monster stories have nothing to do with integrity, courage or brains. Their stock in trade is fear. They take fear of women, fear of father, fear of sexual maturity, fear of blood and mutilation—and we all of us have them all; let nobody kid himself about that. They roll them up in one ball of muck and they hurl them into the reader's face.

Damon Knight has pointed out that characters in such stories do not act rationally—perhaps because if they did, their problems would dissolve. These books are not statements which may be proved true or false. They are exclamations telling us how the writer feels, and not what he thinks. Insofar as they are social criticism they are shrieks: "Everything is bad! I'm frightened by this rotten world! I can't do anything; it's all like a nightmare! Save me, somebody, save me!"

Apparently this wild shriek is deeply meaningful to many people, though not, thank God, to anything like a majority. The proof of this is in the Hollywood box office figures, for the shriek books get made into movies. They do pretty well, but they break no records. If the day ever comes when the shriek movie is a really major type, right up there with, say, the pretentious Western, the implications for the future of democracy will be bad.

I have borrowed some of my material on the "monster" science fiction novel from Chapter 22* of Damon Knight's book *In Search of Wonder.* I want, however, to record my disagreement with his suggestion that the fear in these novels is directed notably against the scientist and intellectual. In this essay I have tried to show that science fiction novels, on the record, have not been measurably effective social criticism. I have speculated that the reason for this is a sort of embarrassment of riches—that nothing in the science fiction novel is what it seems, that there is no starting point for social change resulting from social criticism. As social criticism the science fiction novel is a lever without a fulcrum, a single equation with two unknowns. The science fiction novel does contain social criticism, explicit and implicit, but I believe this criticism is massively outweighed by unconscious symbolic material more concerned with the individual's relationship to his family and the raw universe than with the individual's relationship to society.

In closing, let me say that I would be delighted to be proved wrong in all this. Only with reluctance did I accept the conclusion that science fiction is socially impotent. If it is shown that I am mistaken, I will be the first to cheer at the added stature conferred on a genre of which I am fond.

During the question period that followed delivery of this lecture, some people raised a point which is often expressed as "How do you know you're not reading these things into a story instead of out of it?" At the time I could have given only a rambling answer invoking Occam's Razor, the known complexity of the human brain and a general feeling of "rightness"; actually I evaded the question by saying that it is not compulsory to play the exciting game of modern criticism, and that anybody who does choose to play it must play by the rules.

* Chapter 27 of the revised Second Edition (1967).

I have since learned, however, that there is some experimental evidence for the existence of universal systems of unconscious symbols.

To put it briefly, Smith is hypnotized and told he is undergoing a complicated and fantastic experience. He is then told to dream about the experience and to describe the dream. Jones is then hypnotized and is told to dream the dream described by Smith, which had no apparent similarity to the suggested "experience." Jones is then told to interpret the dream, and he does this by describing the "experience" suggested to Smith. The only communication of the "experience" from Smith to Jones is via the dream, which suggests that Smith and Jones, at least, share a set of unconscious symbols.

I am indebted for this information to Mr. Samuel Randlett of Fisk University. The experiment is described in "An Experimental Approach to Dream Psychology Through Use of Hypnosis," Farber and Fisher, in *Psychoanalytic Quarterly*, Vol. 12, p. 202 (1943).

In addition I want to thank the following people for opinions and suggestions about this work in various stages, without implying that they endorse any or all parts of what I say: Mary Kornbluth, James Blish, A. J. Budrys, Lester and Evelyn del Rey and Frederik Pohl. I owe special thanks to Damon Knight, who appears to be no less than the founder of psychological criticism of science fiction, for originally introducing me to this embattled and fascinating subject.

ALFRED BESTER

science fiction and the renaissance man

I
T'S ALWAYS BEEN A POLICY OF MINE TO
measure a man's opinions against his
background, and if I don't know what
he does for a living, I ask him. This, by the way, is a heinous
crime on the continent. A Parisian or a Roman will discuss
his intimate sex life with you, his religion, politics, prejudices
and sins—but he is offended if you ask questions about his
business. Here in the States, it's the other way around; which
places me in an awkward position because I intend to discuss
both the religion and the business of science fiction. I wish

* Based on a lecture delivered February 22, 1957, University College,
  The University of Chicago.

I could discuss the sex, too, but there isn't any sex in science fiction . . . a deplorable state of affairs.

First, a little about myself so that you can have a yardstick with which to measure my opinions. I'm forty-three years old, married, no children. I was born and raised in New York City . . . on The Rock, as we say . . . meaning on Manhattan Island itself. We have an informal and make-believe snob club of real native New Yorkers. You ought to hear us sneer at the lesser breeds: "My dear! She was born in Brooklyn and raised in the Bronx. She's positively a tourist!"

I was educated in New York public schools; was a science student at the University of Pennsylvania; then a law student at Columbia University. But I was obsessed with the ideal of the Renaissance Man, and spent half my time electing courses in music and art, and slipping my disc winning varsity letters. Naturally I bit off more than I could chew, and never made high enough marks to go on with science and law . . . for which the doctors and lawyers of America have never stopped thanking me. Those were the grim specialist days of the early thirties, before the University of Chicago and St. John's at Annapolis taught our educators to respect and encourage versatility.

I remember I used to rush from the comparative anatomy lab to the art studio, and stink out the life class with a stench of formaldehyde and cadaver. And when I left qualitative analysis for my class in composition and orchestration, bringing with me the sweet scent of sulphur dioxide—! Oh, I tell you, those were miserable days for an amateur Charles van Doren . . . and for his friends, too.

After finishing school, I drifted into writing. Drift is the only word. Put any man at loose ends and he invariably starts to write a book. As a matter of fact if you put a man in jail he also starts to write a book. I don't know if this parallel is significant, but I do know that there are many authors I'd like to see in jail.

The writing that I did was, of course, science fiction. Like every other chess-playing, telescope-loving, microscope-happy teenager of the twenties, I was racked up by the appearance of *Amazing Stories* magazine, Mr. Gernsback's lurid publication. The ideas of fourth dimension, time travel, outer space, microcosm and macrocosm, were fascinating, and I read and loved science fiction until its dissolution into pulp fiction in the thirties disgusted me. It was not until John Campbell rescued it from the abyss of space pirates, mad scientists, their lovely daughters wearing just enough clothes to satisfy the postal authorities, and alien fiends, that I was able to go back to it.

Loving science fiction, steeped in it, and imagining that it was easy to write . . . isn't it astonishing how many people are deceived in this . . . it was only natural that I should attempt to write it. I sold half a dozen miserable stories by the grace of two kindly editors at Standard Magazines who enjoyed discussing James Joyce with me and bought my stories out of pity. When they went over to *Superman Comics*, they took me with them. We hadn't finished *Ulysses* yet. Those were the early days of comic books and they needed stories desperately. I had to forget James Joyce, buckle down and learn to write while they trained me, hammered me, bullied me unmercifully.

But I became a writer, by God! They trained me so well that they lost me. I went over to radio and spent seven years writing and directing clambakes like "Charlie Chan," "Nick Carter," "The Shadow" and so on. When the switch to TV came, I went over to television for another three years, and wrote scripts until I began to dream in camera shots. During all these years I never read science fiction. I had neither the time nor the inclination for it. Make a note of this point. It's important. I'll get back to it later.

The rest of my background is short and hectic. I was contract writer on the Paul Winchell show when Horace Gold

phoned me. I had known him casually in the Squinka days
. . . Squinka is the name Manly Wade Wellman invented for
the scenarios we used to write for comic books . . . Horace
had just started editing *Galaxy* and asked me to write for
him. I laughed hysterically. I knew only too well what a
dreadful science fiction writer I'd been; and anyway I was
putting in a ten day week on my comedy show . . . they're
always a bitch to write . . . and hardly knew what science
fiction meant.

Horace kept calling every week or so, just to chat and
gossip, I thought; but before I realized what that fiend was
up to, he'd maneuvered me into the position that somehow I was obligated to write something for him. Have you
noticed that there's a kind of Machiavelli who can always
put you behind the eight-ball? You're minding your own
business, and the next thing you know you're busting a gut
to do something for the fiend while your common sense is
screaming: "What am I doing here? How'd I get into this?"

The upshot was, I got fired off the Winchell show, went
out to our house on Fire Island, and spent the summer surf-
fishing and writing *The Demolished Man.* I'd read no science
fiction in ten years; I'd written no respectable science fiction
in my entire life; I was convinced I was writing a dog. The
reception of the book surprised and flattered me. But I felt
it was unfair to the professional science fiction authors. I was
(I still am) a science fiction amateur.

After that I wrote a dozen stories for Tony Boucher and
then another novel for Horace Gold: *The Stars My Destination.*

That brings me up to date. I should add that I've tired of
TV now and am making another transition to contemporary
novels and plays. I earn my bread and butter as a columnist
for *Holiday* magazine and *McCall's,* and writing an occasional
Spectacular. Other available data: I'm six-one—weigh two
hundred pounds—am a manic-depressive—a powerful surf-

fisherman—collect 19th century scientific instruments—am always a sucker for a pretty girl, especially if she wears glasses —am emotionally left of center in my politics—and am still trying to live up to my ideal of the Renaissance Man.

One of the most difficult things to teach people outside the arts . . . and in the arts as well . . . is that the important ingredient in the artist is not talent, technique, genius or luck —the important ingredient is himself. What you are must color everything you do. If what you are appeals to your public, you'll be successful. If what you are communicates with all publics through all time, you'll become an immortal. But, if your personality attracts no one, then despite all crafts and cleverness, you'll fail. Perry Lafferty, who directs the Montgomery Show, sums it up bitterly. Perry says: "I'm in the Me business, is all."

Actually this isn't limited to the arts. It extends all through life, and one of the milestones in the maturation of a man is his discovery that technique with women is a waste of time. No matter how he dresses, performs and displays himself, it's only what he really is that attracts.

Hamlet, speaking to the player king, suggests that the goal of the actor should be to hold the mirror up to nature. Actually, no matter what any man does, he holds a mirror up to himself. He continually reveals himself, especially when he tries hardest to conceal himself. All literature reveals authors and readers alike . . . and especially science fiction.

The history of science fiction reflects this. The early *Amazing Stories* magazine was padded with reprints of the work of mature men like H. G. Wells and Jules Verne. This, in part, accounted for the early success of the magazine. Gernsback broke in a half dozen writers who were maladroits as fiction writers but mature experts in one aspect of popular science or another. The maturity of these stone-age science fiction writers was another source of the early success of science fiction. Still another source was the maturity of their themes which were in no way original. Most of their ideas had been waiting around for years for exploitation. Does any reader know the publication date of *Flatland*, by A. Square? Certainly it was centuries before the expression "a square" took on a more sinister meaning.

Within five years science fiction exhausted the reprint field and the prefabricated concepts, and, alas, fell into the hands of the pulp writers. It was then that the great decline set in because science fiction began to reflect the inwardness of the hack writer, and the essence of the hack writer is that he has no inwardness. He has no contact with reality, no sense of dramatic proportion, no principles of human behavior, no eye for truth . . . and a wooden ear for dialogue. He is all compromise and clever-shabby tricks.

For nearly ten years science fiction wallowed in this pig sty while the faithful complained pathetically. The fans pleaded with the editors. They also berated the editors, never once realizing that the inwardness of the writers was to blame . . . not their stories, which were sometimes well-made, with every clever-shabby trick known to the craft . . . but their empty inwardness. Many empty men wrote clever, gimmicky stories that still left the readers feeling dissatisfied. They had nothing within themselves to communicate.

Now you mustn't confuse inwardness with purpose or a message. When I say a man has nothing to communicate, I don't mean he has no message to preach. No. I'm referring to a quality we sometimes call character or charm . . . a point of view, an attitude toward life that is interesting or attractive. And remember that everybody has character, in varying degrees. Also remember that only the unique individuals have charm for everybody else. How often does an Audrey Hepburn come along? Or, if you prefer, a Rosemary Clooney? Or, for the ladies, a Rex Harrison? No, most of us must be content with a Charm Quotient . . . a CQ . . . of less than one hundred.

Back in the thirties we used to wonder why we enjoyed Doc Smith's space-operas so much. We usually felt guilty about it. Now I realize that Doc Smith had charm for us then. There was something inside him, reflected in his stereotype blood and thunder, that appealed. How many times, writing and directing my own shows, have I seen the same miracle transform actors . . . miserable technicians with no acting talent at all, and yet exuding a charm that was worth all the deficiencies. Fellow-sufferers, if you ever have the choice between a high IQ or a high CQ, I urge you to settle for charm.

John W. Campbell, Jr. was the man who rescued science fiction from the emptiness. Now Campbell is a strange man . . . from all reports. I only met him once, when he was embarking on his Dianetics kick, and my experience with him was laughable and embarrassing. But strange though Campbell may be, he's a man with a forceful inwardness which immediately shone through the pages of *Astounding Science Fiction*. I think in Campbell's case, the inwardness was character rather than charm.

Later came Horace Gold of *Galaxy* and Tony Boucher of *Fantasy and Science Fiction*. Like Campbell, Gold and Boucher are strange men; also like Campbell, both have a forceful inwardness which is reflected in their magazines. And remember, there aren't so many men who have forceful inwardness, strange or otherwise.

Campbell gave science fiction character; Gold and Boucher broadened its horizons. The hack writers began to disappear; the honest craftsmen who had been forced to hack in order to conform were able to do honest work again; new writers emerged. Science fiction began to create new concepts because new minds, minds in depth, so to speak, were attracted to it. It began to appeal again because new personalities, personalities in depth, were communicating through the stories . . . Heinlein, Kuttner, van Vogt, Sturgeon, Asimov, Kornbluth. These men fascinated us . . . but how much, really? Now I come to the heretical part of this essay. All traditionalists and royalists should be cautioned before reading further.

Do you remember my telling you that during the ten year period when I was writing and directing shows, I lost all interest in science fiction? Let me describe how and why.

Picture to yourself a Monday in the life of Me. I'm writing a show called . . . oh, say, "Secret Service." Monday morning at 9:00 o'clock I finish a 48 hour drive without letup to complete my script for the show three weeks from today. The network has been badgering me for the script which was due last Friday, and threatening to hire another writer. I call a messenger service to rush it down to the network and suffer because it's the only copy. I was too rushed to type a carbon.

The client on "Secret Service" calls to tell me that the script for the show two weeks from today has been unconditionally rejected by his wife. I fight desperately to salvage something out of the disaster. The advertising agency calls to tell me that next week's show must be postponed because of an advertising promotion they've dreamed up, and I have to get a new script written in three days. Also it must integrate with the promotion. The casting director of "Secret Service" calls to announce that one of the bit-players for tonight's show is out with a virus and they can't recast and rehearse on short notice. Can I write the part out?

I go down to the network and rewrite, fighting haggardly with the director, a compulsive man who can't feel comfortable unless he's dominating all situations, but who can't respect a colleague unless the colleague fights him to a standstill. I walk a neurotic tightrope with him while I try to make sense out of a script minus a character.

In the studio during rehearsal I discover that a dramatic turning point in the story can't be done because of a jurisdictional fight between the stagehands' union and the carpenters' union. I'm a strong union man myself, but at this moment I would cheerfully set fire to the A.F. of L. But after losing a fight with the shop stewards, I restrain my fury and try to come up with something valid and dramatic to replace the device that only took me two weeks to figure out.

At dress rehearsal, the director and cast begin screaming at each other and at me. "You let us down!" they wail. If a show stinks, it's the writer's fault. If it's a success, it was despite the script. When in doubt, persecute the writer. I'm too weary to defend myself, and besides, the client's wife, a bright woman who knows she could write brilliantly if she only had the time, is busy discussing Kafka with me. I loathe Kafka, but I have to be polite. I even have to listen.

I drink too much after the show, out of relief and hysteria. I hear rumors that we're going to be cancelled, and I suffer. I go home and find a letter from my accountant. I owe more money to the government. I'm too overwrought to sleep. I take two sleeping pills and settle down with a science fiction magazine . . . And make the strange discovery that I'm not a damned bit interested in a make-believe story about an inventor who tries to ride a rocket to the moon and only succeeds in destroying the Earth, and worries that now he's Adam but there's no Eve to help him repopulate the world, only he does it all by himself anyway.

In the entertainment business, life is constant conflict . . . all tension and dynamics, which is why we consume so many Miltowns, Nembutals and head-doctors. But all life is conflict, tension and dynamics. You must go through what I go through; perhaps not so often, perhaps not continually, but it happens to you. The point I'm making is this: When I'm most at grips with dramatic reality, I have the least interest in science fiction. I suggest the same is true of yourselves . . . of everybody.

This doesn't hold for all literature. I don't mean that when one is closest to reality one gives up all reading entirely. On the contrary, some books become more necessary than Miltowns when one is deeply embroiled in conflicts. What I'm suggesting is this: that science fiction is a form of literature palatable only in our moments of leisure, calm, euphoria. It's not Escape Fiction; it's Arrest Fiction. I use the word "arrest" in the sense of arresting or striking attention . . . to excite, stimulate, enlarge. No one wants to read Arrest Fiction when he's already excited; we can only enjoy it when we're calm and euphoric.

Euphoria is a generalized feeling of well-being, not amounting to a definite effect of gladness. I use it here with particular reference to adults. To be blunt, only a man who's known adult troubles can know the meaning of euphoria. Young people—and I was a young people myself once—know all the agony of youth and experience moments of relief; but that isn't adult trouble or adult euphoria.

Young people often withdraw into unadulterated escape fiction, including science fiction. They also engulf science fiction along with everything else as a part of the omnivorous curiosity of youth. Arrested adults . . . that is, arrested in development, also withdraw into unadulterated escape fiction, including science fiction; but we're not discussing the youthful and/or withdrawn readers of science fiction here. We're discussing the mature fans who enjoy science fiction just as they enjoy hi-fi, art, politics, sports, escape fiction, serious reading, mischief and hard work . . . all in sensible proportions, depending upon opportunity, season and mood. I contend that science fiction is only for the euphoric mood.

I think the strongest support for my contention is the fact that women, as a rule, are not fond of science fiction. The reason for this is obvious . . . at least to me. Woman are basically realists; men are the romantics. The hard core of realism in women usually stifles the Cloud Nine condition necessary for the enjoyment of science fiction. When a woman dreams, she extrapolates reality; her fantasies are always based on fact. Women's magazines . . . and I speak as a *McCall's* writer

... devote themselves to fantasies about love, marriage and the home, not contra-terrene matter. And the writers who appeal to them are those writers whose inwardness reflects an attitude about love, marriage and the home that is attractive to women.

What, then, is the inwardness of science fiction writers that appeals to fans when they are calm and euphoric? Let's immediately dismiss all notions of serious social criticism, valuable scientific speculation, important philosophic extrapolation, and so on. These are the pretences of science fiction and they're really worthless. But since I know you won't let me dismiss them as externals without an argument, I'll speak about them for a moment before I go on with euphoria.

So far as the philosophic contribution of science fiction is concerned, I cite the gag that made the rounds last fall about the couple that'd been married fifty years. You all know it, but I'll tell it anyway; I've got you trapped. They were interviewed and the husband was asked the secret of the happy marriage. He said: "When we got married we decided that my wife would make all the little decisions, and I'd make the big decisions." The interviewer asked: "What are the little decisions?" "Oh, what apartment to rent. How much rent to pay. Should I keep my job. Should I ask for a raise. What school to send the children to ... Things like that." "And what are the big decisions?" "Oh ... who to run for president. What to do about the Far East. Should we help Slobbovia."

Translating this into science fiction, it's my claim that when it comes to social criticism, philosophy and so on, science fiction is usually making the big decision. It knows little and cares less about the day-to-day working out of the details of reality; it's only interested in making the big decisions: Who to run for galactic president. What to do about Mars. Should we help Alpha Centauri.

So far as the scientific contribution of science fiction is

concerned, I'm going to tell you the Pshush Story whether you like it or not. During the war, an Admiral was going through some personnel records and on one man's sheet he found the entry: Civilian Occupation—Pshush-Maker. In those days everybody was looking for a secret weapon, so the Admiral called the man in and said: "It says here you're a Pshush-Maker. What's a Pshush-Maker?" The man said: "I can't explain; I'll have to show you, sir." The Admiral said: "What d'you need?" The man said: "Fifty-seven men and a corvette."

So they gave him the fifty-seven men and the corvette, and he spent three months sailing around the world gathering rare materials . . . copper, silver, platinum, rock crystal, aluminum ore, and so on. Then he gave a top-secret demonstration up in Baffin Bay. The Admiral was there and more top brass, and they watched the fifty-seven men put all those materials together into a huge contraption on the stern of the corvette. Then they lit blow-torches and heated it white hot. And then they pushed it over the stern . . . and it went: *PSHUSH!*

The science in science fiction is usually Pshush-Making. We gather rare materials . . . the theories, ideas and speculations of genuine scientists . . . we put them together in strange contraptions . . . we heat them white hot with the talent and technique of the professional writer . . . and all for what? To make a huge Pshush! If the Admiral had gone into a serious conference with his top brass to discuss the military value of Pshush-Making, it would be no more ridiculous than discussing the serious scientific aspects of science fiction.

But there's a silver lining . . . or should I say a Pshush-Lining . . . to the cloud, because it's my contention that this is the essential charm of science fiction. I said before that men are the romantics. Unlike women, we can't find perpetual pleasure in the day-to-day details of living. A woman can come home ecstatic because she bought a three-dollar item reduced to two-eighty-seven, but a man needs more.

Every so often, when we're temporarily freed from conflicts
. . . euphoric, if you please . . . we like to settle down for a
few hours and ask why we're living and where we're going.
Life is enough for most women; most thinking men must ask
why and whither.

In England men have the pub for this. You can spend a
few hours in your local, talking up a storm with other men
about why and whither. Alfred Doolittle, Bernard Shaw's
dustman in *Pygmalion* is the supreme example. In France
they quonk all day in the street cafes. In Italy they have the
coffee bars, and in Vienna the weinstubes. Here in the States
the thinking man has nothing. After the joys of the college
bull-session (Is it still called bull-session?) there's nowhere to
go. Nobody talks in American saloons; everybody's too busy
trying to imitate Steve Allen or Arthur Godfrey. And anyway, too many American men are compulsives, too driven
by their hysterias to be capable of euphoric talk. What other
outlet does the thinking man have in his hours of reflection
but science fiction?

No . . . If you love me and if you love science fiction, deliver us both from all implications of scientific significance.
Deliver science fiction from any necessity to have purpose
and value. Science fiction is far above the utilitarian yard-
sticks of the technical minds, the agency minds, the teaching
minds. Science fiction is not for Squares. It's for the modern
Renaissance Man . . . vigorous, versatile, zestful . . . full of romantic curiosity and impractical speculation.

Haven't I just drawn a picture of the inwardness of the
science fiction writers who appeal to you? What have any
of them contributed to modern science, philosophy, sociology, criticism? Nothing, thank God. They've been writing
Arrest Fiction, which strikes your attention, excites, stimu-
lates and enlarges you when you're in the mood to be excited
and stimulated . . . when you're in the euphoric mood and
eager to be excited, stimulated and enlarged.

When I want an education, I don't go to Heinlein, Kuttner, van Vogt, Sturgeon, et alios. I go to grim texts by experts and learn while I work and suffer. But when I want the joy of communicating with other Renaissance Men, I abandon the Squares and go to Heinlein, Kuttner, van Vogt, et alios. These are the men I love to speculate with in my local pub, while my wife is home counting the laundry.

Let me be specific. I am, as I indicated, an amateur in science fiction. My real writing trade lies in other fields. I've only met a few of the leading science fiction writers, but their characters bear out my argument in their work. Bob Heinlein's extrapolation of the future of our civilization is ingenious, imaginative and worthless. But Bob has a dry, wry approach to life that is reflected in all his writing and is a joy to be with. You can say what you like about his science, but the fact remains that he's the Will Rogers of science fiction, and an ideal companion for a pub.

Ted Sturgeon is an imaginative, sensitive poet who can write about human emotions with so much power that he's wasted in science fiction. His science is plausibly makeshift; his fiction is unique. His understanding and approach to human beings . . . his CQ, if you please . . . makes him too touching to be endured. Like Heinlein, Sturgeon has within himself too much to be squandered on a form of fiction which, by its very framework, is dedicated solely to our hours of euphoria.

What about me? Alfie Bester. Now we get down to basics. What made *The Demolished Man* an appealing book, whereas the stories I'd written ten years before were appalling drivel? The answer is: Ten years. I was ten years older; ten years more experienced. Ten years of hard work at grips with hard reality crystallized something within me and gave me an attitude. I didn't realize it then, but ten years had turned me from a boy into a man.

I think I understand what you liked about *The Demolished*

Man. Outside the tricks and gimmicks which any good crafts-man can come up with ... what you liked was what was within myself; my attitude toward people and life. It wasn't my thinking that you liked, no matter what you tell your-self. I can't think my way out of a telephone booth. It was my formed emotional attitude that communicated with you. I told you I was emotionally left of center in my politics; the same is true of my attitude toward people.

I believe that everyone is compelled, but no one is bad. I believe that everyone has greatness in him, but few of us have the opportunity to fulfill ourselves. I believe that every-one has love in him, but most of our loves are frustrated. I believe that man is the unique creation of nature, but am capable of believing in an even more perfect creation. I be-lieve that every hope and aspiration, and every weakness and vice that I have, I share with all my brothers in the world ... and all the world is my brother.

All this is emotional, without validity and without value to anyone looking for scientific data and rules to regulate his life. But I feel I'm the kind of guy you wouldn't mind spending a few hours with in a saloon, talking up a storm about anything ... Exactly the way you'd like to spend time with a Heinlein or a Sturgeon. That's the appeal of *The De-molished Man.* Not what I say, but what compelled me to say the things I said.

I speak to you now as a brother in a rather unique position; I'm capable of honesty. The only things that stand between a man and honesty are the symbols of his youth which must be fulfilled and discharged. A hungry man can't be honest. I've been fortunate enough to have purged myself of most of my adolescent obsessions. I can afford to be honest today because I've been lucky enough to have had all those things that can only be obtained through dishonesty. I've had them and I'm through with them. Only integrity remains. Now then:

Should we take science fiction seriously?

No more or less than we take television seriously.

Why?

Because both are of limited framework; and any art form of limited framework calls to itself limited artists and is worth only limited consideration.

What is the purpose of art?

To entertain and/or move the audience.

Can science fiction entertain?

Yes, when we're in certain receptive moods.

Can it move us?

No.

Why?

I can only answer that question by committing the heinous crime of discussing your literary religion. And the best way to begin is to mention Ignatius Donnelly, the patron saint of American readers . . . although very few know his name. Donnelly wrote a book called *The Great Cryptogram.* Does that ring a bell? It was Mr. Donnelly who tried to prove that Bacon wrote Shakespeare.

He's the patron saint of American readers because few American readers really believe that Shakespeare wrote Shakespeare. Few Americans can comprehend or understand artistic genius. Faced with unique achievement in the arts, Americans always poke around behind the scenes, looking for ghost writers, the unknown collaborator, the hidden power behind the throne. It never seems to occur to them that once they've found the hidden power, they'll come up against the same problem all over again, and have to poke around ad infinitum.

Now it's interesting that Americans never feel this way about science. No one has ever written a book trying to prove that somebody else invented Edison's inventions. Nobody ever digs up Morse's grave to see if he really invented Marconi's wireless. There's an ancient superstition that an unknown Negro writes Irving Berlin's music, but no one dreams that a Japanese invented the airplane for the Wright brothers. Oh, it's true that scientists sometimes get into priority hassles, but no American is ever incapable of comprehending scientific genius. The reason is that we're a nation of amateur mechanics. We're simpatico to science and invention, and can identify with mechanical genius. Four Americans out of every five are nursing a secret invention, and take this dream quite seriously. I'm still convinced that da Vinci is a popular painter with us mainly because of the appeal of his beautiful mechanical drawings. I'm also convinced that photography became a passion with us because it made it possible to simulate creative results through purely mechanical means.

I hope you don't know the story about the two amateur photographers who met in a darkroom. One said to the other: "Gee, I saw a pathetic sight in the park today. It was an old beggar, with a long white beard and shaggy hair. His clothes were torn; he was dirty and starved; and the hand he held out to me looked like a claw." The second amateur said: "What'd you give him?" "Oh, a fiftieth of a second at f:3.5."

In a sense this is the American attitude toward the human scene. We're interested in aperture and shutter speed, time and temperature control. We're interested in the mechanics of the human being . . . his anatomy, morphology and psychology; the statistics of his life, death and mating habits . . . but we're not really interested in human beings as humanity . . . as fellow creatures. It's this fact, by the way, that accounts for the perennial popularity of the so-called situation comedy in stage, screen and television. I don't have to point out that situation comedies concentrate on the mechanics of a situation rather than the human beings involved in it.

Since art, literature and poetry are concerned with the human being as a fellow creature . . . almost a part or reflection of ourselves . . . we're not very sympathetic to them or to their great craftsmen. This is why we find it difficult to understand the artistic genius. It is also why we prefer our science fiction to concentrate on the mechanics of life and leave human beings alone.

Science fiction rarely, if ever, deals with genuine human emotions and problems. Its science ranges from the 20th to the 50th century A.D. Its characters usually remain back in the 16th century A.D. They are drawn in the two-dimensional style of the Morality Plays, and they face problems of horse-opera depth. When science fiction attempts comedy . . . which is the essence of humanity . . . it only succeeds in belaboring itself with empty bladders.

Any art form which studiously avoids human reality as a subject can't hope to move its audience. Science fiction can entertain and intrigue us, stimulate and enlarge us with its novel ideas and ingenious extrapolations, but it can rarely move us to pity and terror. There are exceptions, of course . . . but in general, science fiction suffers from high emotional vacuum.

You may argue: "Granting what you say is true, what difference does that make? Must literature move its readers to pity and terror to be respectable? Isn't there such a thing as escape, or arrest-fiction?"

I answer: "You're absolutely right. There is such a thing as escape fiction, and I'm not pretending to pass on the respectability of any form of literature. I'm merely trying to place science fiction in terms of authors, themes and readers, with emphasis at this point upon the reader."

A drama professor of mine once asked our class what we thought was the central fact, the essence of the theater. We suggested the stage itself . . . the actors . . . the author's script . . . He told us we were wrong. The essence of the theater is the audience. The audience shares a play in its making. The theater is never a living thing until it is shared.

Anyone who's ever been to the theater or worked on stage knows this is true. You must have experienced that sharing communication between cast and audience that brings the theater to life. This sharing is the crucial reason why radio, television and motion pictures tire an audience, whereas the theater does not. You can't communicate with un-dead things, they exhaust you. Only communication can inspire and energize.

There is, alas, no such communication between novelist and reader, but there is a form of it existing between a school of literature and its followers. The school of science fiction and its fans do communicate with each other, influence each other, and even to some degree by telepathy, or diabolic possession . . . but I know it does happen.

I've had this in mind all the while I've been speaking so frankly about science fiction; not . . . so help me . . . in order to preach a message and turn you into crusaders for the betterment of the craft. I wouldn't know which direction was the direction myself. No. I've been quonking like this in hope that it will enable us to understand ourselves and share each other a little better . . . authors and readers alike.

Science fiction, like all the arts, like every living act of man, is a mirror of ourselves. If we can understand science fiction, without delusions, recriminations, attacks and defenses, we may be able to understand ourselves . . . and vice versa. That old Renaissance cat that I'm always dangling before my conscience tried to understand without judging. We should do the same.

What are we, then, in terms of science fiction? What is science fiction in terms of us? Let me piece the picture together for you; and remember that it's only a part of ourselves. It's a picture of a passionate young romantic who runs away from his soul and focusses his passion on the objective world . . . a romantic with the courage to entertain daring and complex concepts, yet who is afraid of the per-

plexities of human behavior . . . a romantic full of curiosity,
yet curiously indifferent to half the marvels around him . . .
a romantic; vigorous and honest in his speculations, yet
often deluding himself as to the value of his speculations . . .
a charming romantic, but a withdrawn romantic . . . a Renaissance romantic, but a neurotic romantic.

This is my picture of science fiction, of you, of myself.
If you don't like the portrait, you can argue with me, of
course; but I'd suggest instead that you use a line reported
by S. N. Behrman. When Behrman was a boy in Providence,
Rhode Island, one of the most eminent men in the city was
Dr. Bradley, president of Brown University. One afternoon,
Behrman took a trolleycar in town and saw Dr. Bradley sit-
ting down the aisle. In front of the doctor stood four orthodox rabbis, examining the embarrassed gentleman and arguing
furiously in Yiddish whether this was the great man or not.
Finally they turned to Behrman and one of them asked: "Is
that man the brilliant scholar, Doctor Bradley?" Behrman
said it was. The rabbi started in disappointment and then
said: "Well . . . If that man is Dr. Bradley, then anybody
could be anybody."

ROBERT BLOCH

imagination and modern social criticism

I WONDER HOW MANY OF YOU REALIZE JUST
how horrible it was to be a child, thirty
years ago.

There was absolutely nothing for a youngster to do, because nobody owned a television set.

A growing boy had no way of enjoying life, since juvenile delinquency hadn't even been invented yet.

As a result, many children were driven, in sheer desperation, to taking up reading.

This in itself is a dreadful fate to contemplate, but in

---

* Based on a lecture delivered March 8, 1957, University College, The University of Chicago.

actuality it was even worse than you might imagine. You see, thirty years ago there weren't any comic books. And poor, innocent little kiddies were forced to read great big volumes, with scarcely any pictures in them, and lots of hard, two-syllable words.

No, it wasn't easy to be a child thirty years ago, and I ought to know. At the time I was nine years old, and residing in the peaceful little Chicago suburb of Maywood. And it was there that I found myself trapped inside the public library. To make matters worse, I soon exhausted its selection of Oz books, *Dr. Dolittle* and *A Boy's Life of Al Capone*. I was forced to ask permission to take books from the adult section. From thence forward, my doom was sealed. I became a constant, almost a chronic, reader. I couldn't shake the habit—I had a monkey on my back in the form of a thirty-seven-pound Unabridged Dictionary.

And the things I read were vile; hideous, corrupt trash written by notorious eggheads, liberals and other Communists. You could tell they were Communists because their books were always criticizing the status quo.

I remember some woman named Harriet Beecher Stowe who had the nerve to come out denouncing slavery, way back in the 1850's. Denouncing slavery, mind you, at a time when that institution was a recognized part of our glorious national heritage!

Then there was a fellow named Mark Twain, who sort of poked fun at politicians and southern aristocrats and small town people. I guess he was trying to be funny, like this Finley Peter Dunne, who wrote of Mr. Dooley and made jokes about war and the government. Another writer, Ring Lardner, attacked just about everybody, including prize-fight champions, and even went so far as to hint that baseball players are sometimes pretty stupid. And there was a magazine put out by some wild-eyed radical named Mencken: I wouldn't even dare repeat some of the things he said. He

even criticized President Coolidge! And he was against Prohibition, too, just as if it weren't right smack part of our own
Constitution.

Today, of course, everybody knows that a humorist is a
man who writes little pieces in the back of magazines or
newspaper sections telling about how dumb all fathers are,
and how their kids get the best of them, and how tough it is
to mow the lawn and do the housework when their wives are
gone. That's American humor today, and we all love it and
get many a chuckle out of dear old Dad.

But in those far-off times humor was simply a fright. You
never knew what some of these men would say next. There
was even somebody called Will Rogers who spent most of
his time ridiculing Congress; it's lucky for him there wasn't
a Senator McCarthy around to give him a good Loyalty
Quiz.

Now I know it must disturb you to hear about such un-
pleasant things, but it's my duty to tell you there were even
worse books current.

Theodore Dreiser was writing about great financiers, and
trying to make out that some of them were just crooks and
grafters. Sinclair Lewis claimed that life in small towns was
often dull and stupid, and that big city businessmen weren't
as smart as they made out to be. And he said there was some
corruption in medical circles, and that certain ministers were
hypocrites. A fellow named Upton Sinclair wrote attacks on
all kinds of professions—he even went after the newspapers!
Why, believe it or not, Sinclair had the nerve to criticize the
stockyards! Nothing was sacred.

Oh, it was shocking, the kind of thing they published in
those days—and the Depression only made the situation
worse. James T. Farrell wrote nasty stories about Chicago,
and John Dos Passos wrote nasty stories about the whole
U.S.A., and John Steinbeck criticized the way the Okies were
treated.

Where it all might have ended, it's hard to say. Fortunately, however, it doesn't much matter, because today's children don't need to waste their time on books any more. Now we have television in every tavern, and plenty of rock-and-roll and hot-rods and universal military training and all sorts of modern amusements.

And even if young people still were reading books today, I can assure you there'd be little danger in the habit. Because, along about the time of World War II, books changed.

Writers suddenly woke up to reality and forgot all this stupid criticism. Upton Sinclair quit his bellyaching and began a long series about a patriotic young man named Lanny Budd. Sinclair Lewis took back what he'd said about Babbitt and Main Street. And a whole group of new writers came along with a series of great and inspiring messages.

All you have to do is take a look at a recent crop of best-selling novels to see what I mean.

There's *The Caine Mutiny*, which teaches us it's wrong to disobey the Captain or go around thinking he's crazy, if we want to get along in the Navy. And *From Here to Eternity*, which doesn't pull any punches—it admits life in the Army can be tough, but the important thing is discipline and learning to love the system. And *Not as a Stranger*, which is about doctors—in fact its plot sounds a lot like a book Sinclair Lewis wrote in the Bad Old Days, except that it shows most doctors are dedicated and live up to all the principles of the American Medical Association, just like it says in *Hygeia* magazine.

And even better, there are those books about businessmen —*Executive Suite* and *The Man in the Gray Flannel Suit* and *Cash McCall*, which prove that big businessmen really do their best for the country, and, like the old saying has it, "What's good for General Motors is good for the nation."

Finally, *The Last Hurrah*, which shows us that so-called "machine politics" and political bosses are pretty darned swell, because you have to be practical about such things.

So you see, the tide has turned. Even Philip Wylie, who was always griping about "Mom," has turned around and admitted that "Mom" is a pretty Grand Old Girl after all. Nowadays Mr. Wylie spends his time working on Civil Defense and he's stopped most of this nonsense about rebellion. Like many psychotherapists today, he sees that most people wouldn't have any of their so-called "troubles" if they'd just learn to stay in line and stop complaining or trying to be "individualists." We're gradually learning that we must adapt, we must conform to the rules instead of wasting our time and energy asking a lot of foolish questions or putting up a bunch of stupid arguments.

Yes, modern social criticism—adverse, that is—seems just about dead. There's just one place where you're still likely to run into it; and in a form of writing so minor that most serious literary reviewers aren't even aware of it.

I refer, of course, to the field of science fiction. Now when I was a child, science fiction was different, too. Back in the late twenties and early thirties, science fiction was a field in which stories about Bug-Eyed Monsters were read by bug-eyed boys. It was full of crazy stuff about airplanes going faster than the speed of sound . . . and splitting the atom to harness its energy . . . and space-platforms hanging out in the middle of nowhere above the Earth. Just pulp trash, the product of diseased imaginations. Of course, nobody took it seriously.

But something happened, along about the time of World War II. Maybe it was the atomic bomb; maybe there is something to this idea that radiation and fallout can affect people in mysterious ways. At any rate, it affected our main-stream writers and caused them to begin producing wonderful new stories in praise of the status quo. And at the same time, it seemingly caused science fiction writers to suddenly emerge as rebels and prophets.

Science fiction became the vehicle for social criticism.

Right now we're going to take a look at that vehicle. We're going to kick its tires, tinker with its ignition, try to peer under the hood to squint at its motor and its motive-power, and above all, consider where this vehicle is headed. In what direction is it trying to take us?

The old Model A science fiction, with its universal gear-shift and universal space-time shift, operated in company with a road-map to Terra Incognita: it directed us to the realms of imagination.

Today's streamlined conveyance transports us to the worlds of our own possible future. It offers a more up-to-date and realistic road-map, filled with landmarks we all recognize; points out certain detours, certain extensions of our present known highways which, if taken, can lead us to heavens above or along the well-paved road to hell on earth.

When I learned I was to deal with the topic of science fiction novels in terms of imagination and modern social criticism, I prepared for the task by re-reading fifty of these books. I deliberately picked titles at random, in order to get a more or less average cross-section of available contemporary material. My only rule was to stick to novels with a pre-ponderantly mundane setting.

As I read, I tried to divide the novels into three ancient and elementary categories according to their themes: Man Against Nature, Man Against Himself and Man Against Man.

The Man Against Nature books would include, by extended definition, novels dealing primarily with extrapolation of so-called "natural laws"—such as H. G. Wells' *The Time Machine*. Plus, of course, books revolving around invasions of extra-terrestrials, or the ravages of plague or atomic destruction.

In this category I placed: *The Time Machine, Twenty Thousand Leagues Under the Sea, Day of the Triffids, Out of the Deeps, The Puppet Masters, Sinister Barrier, Child-*

hood's End, War With the Newts, The Long Loud Silence, Nutro 29, Greener Than You Think, The Body Snatchers and *I Am Thinking of My Darling.*

Considering the theme of Man Against Himself, I encountered *More Than Human, The Demolished Man* and *1984.*

So far the count was sixteen titles in the first two categories. But of these sixteen, only the Wells and the Verne novels were primarily unified. The remaining fourteen all had strong elements of Man Against Man in them.

And the other thirty-five books I considered were unmistakably in this grouping. I'll list the titles at random, in the hope that some, if not all, are familiar to you: *Wild Talent, The Lights in the Sky Are Stars, Hell's Pavement, The Syndic, Gladiator-At-Law, Not This August, Brave New World, The Golden Kazoo, Bring the Jubilee, The Space Merchants, The Secret Masters, Brain Wave, Fahrenheit 451, Space Cadet, Messiah, Reprieve From Paradise, This Fortress World, Gather, Darkness!, The Big Ball of Wax, Player Piano, Highways in Hiding, The Lovers, Limbo, Ape and Essence, Odd John, Doctor Arnoldi, Preferred Risk, The Power, Revolt in 2100, Beyond This Horizon, The Humanoids, The Caves of Steel, You Shall Know Them, Tiger! Tiger! (The Stars My Destination),* and *The Door Into Summer.*

Their over-all basic theme? Man Against Man. Here is opportunity for social criticism with a vengeance.

And just how does this wide assortment of writers view the world of the present and the extrapolated society of the future? Ignoring the extra-terrestrial invaders, ignoring the gadgetry, ignoring the universal-disaster backgrounds, one encounters a fundamental dramatic premise known to all eminent critics who are six years old or over. The world is plainly divided into "cops and robbers," "cowboys and Indians" or "good guys and bad guys."

There's a reason, of course. People who have come to revere science almost as a religion place great faith in the ability of technologists to safeguard our future. Many of these people had that faith literally exploded with the explosion of the atomic bomb. Science fiction has attempted to shore up that faith once more with something called the "upbeat" story—one in which science, despite the danger of thermonuclear destruction, triumphs in the end and restores a brave new world. Sometimes these stories are quite deceptively satirical and begin in an atmosphere of tyranny. But if you read further, you're apt to encounter the same old hero, learning the error of his ways and overthrowing the tyrants. There are minor variations, of course: in *Brave New World* and *1984*, for example, the heroes fail—and the point is, you can't beat the system. In one or two books the authors, seeking for novelty, invert the premise at the end and we discover that the system is right after all—whereupon the hero wisely concludes that if you can't lick 'em, join 'em.

No wonder so many adolescents are attracted to this form of fiction; here, in a transparent disguise, is the story of revolt against organized society. The hero—with whom the adolescent identifies—defies the rules and the taboos and the authorities.

In an era where "escape fiction" cannot serve up a convincing trip to the Wild West or an exploration of Darkest Africa as a refuge against social constraints, our adolescents revel in spaceships breaking free to seek the stars, and in contradictions of supposedly immutable order. There's a vicarious thrill in breaking the law, even if it's the law of gravity.

But surprisingly few of these concepts dominate contemporary science fiction novels. The E. E. Smith gallivantings through the galaxies have given place to an exploration of more mundane pathways—to say nothing of psychopathways.

While main-stream fiction glorifies the status quo, science fiction seemingly singles it out as the villain. And at the same time it presents us with the reassuring Father-Image of the all-wise scientist and psychotherapist. With his aid, the hero triumphs. Science fiction thus reassures people that they are the masters of their fate, and that every mushroom cloud has a silver lining.

Now this is admittedly a generalization, and there are notable exceptions. Among the novels I listed, one can pick out such memorable character-delineations as Tucker's *The Long Loud Silence*, Vidal's *Messiah* and Moore's *Greener Than You Think*, for example.

But by far the majority adhere to that stereotyped concept—the Hero Who Saves the World.

Here is Doctor Martine, hero of *Limbo*: the brilliant scientist incarnate, who single-handedly seeks to rescue the world from a social order he himself unwittingly imposed upon it. Here is Doctor Paul Proteus of *Player Piano*, not too different in his attitude from those other famous medicos, Doctor Kildare, Doctor Christian and Young Doctor Malone.

Mitch Courtenay of *The Space Merchants* is no M.D., but a willing conformist—until the scales are stripped from his eyes and he takes a good look at the society around him—whereupon he realizes that it is his mission in life, too, to Fight Tyranny. Does this begin to sound familiar? Have you read about this hero before—in Edson McCann's *Preferred Risk*, in Damon Knight's *Hell's Pavement* and heaven knows how many other books?

But note this well: I'm not decrying such heroes, as such. I'm not ridiculing lofty motives, or the device of allowing a conformist character to rebel against what he discovers to be a false system of values. The device of casting down the mighty and making them realize how conditions are under slavery was good enough for Mark Twain in *A Connecticut Yankee in King Arthur's Court*; this is sound plotting, and the result, properly handled, can be a realistic and convincing story.

Yet in many of these novels, something is off-key. Can it be—I wonder—that the heroes are too important?

That's where some of these books destroy the illusion of reality for me. I'm transported right back to the days of Hugo Gernsback where, in many instances, the handsome but brilliant young fullback landed on Mars and immediately found himself involved with the Princess, the High Priest and the Emperor. By the time you reached the fourth page of such epics, Our Boy was always tangling with the highest figures in the Hierarchy, and he and he alone eventually decided the fate and future of the planet, the galaxy or the entire universe.

And here we are again today. Sophisticated superimpositions of satire, sophistry, sociology and psychiatry notwithstanding, there's one basic plot—Boy Meets Big Wheel, and overturns the world.

Now the thing that made *1984* a convincing tour-de-force was its depiction of an average citizen against an average background. It was not necessary for Orwell to pit his commonplace hero against the Top Dogs in order to make a plot and a point. Indeed, the strength and the conviction of his book lies in the way he deliberately offers a "slice of life" rather than an orgy of name-dropping.

Is there a sound sociological reason why so much of science fiction must concern itself with so-called Key Figures? It is certainly not a criminal offense to do so, but to some extent I believe it is a literary offense. Because in science fiction novels which are deliberately presented as glimpses of our possible society of tomorrow, the writer is in effect offering a promise to the reader. He is saying, "Come with me and I'll show you how the world of the future will be—the kind of people who live there, what they think, and what effect tomorrow's social order will have upon them."

In *1984*, Orwell did just that. But in the average tale of tomorrow, the author goes straight to the top. He may make grudging mention of the lower classes or even present picturesque (and usually criminal) specimens in one or two chapters — but the greater part of his book usually offers glimpses of Important Officials Guiding Destiny and Revealing Their Philosophy. The heroes and their peers seem just a bit larger than life-sized, and you seldom come away from your reading with the feeling of, "Yes, this is how it really could be."

You may, if the author is skillful — and many of them are — enjoy sharing the experience and the danger, and revel in the hero's eventual triumph. But your attention has been directed away from the theme and centered upon the gaudy melodrama of Intrigue in High Places.

It's fun to read about d'Artagnan and the Queen — but you don't go to *The Three Musketeers* to find out how life was actually lived in the days of the French Monarchy.

Science fiction as a vehicle for social criticism is stalled when one of those super-heroes climbs into the driver's seat and insists on racing full-speed-ahead right down the center of the main highway. You're so busy watching for the possibility of accidents and smashups that you never really see the scenery. Thrilling? Yes. Contemplative? Hardly.

But suppose we make the best of things and decide we're going to put up with a dare-devil driver if we want to get anywhere. And suppose we steel ourselves to ignore the danger-signals and the cleverly-prepared barricades and obstacles set up by the author and glue our eyes to the social scene through which his hero leads us.

What kind of a future society does the average science fiction novelist extrapolate for our consideration?

In general, we can count on some — or all — of the following ingredients:

1. A TOTALITARIAN STATE. Maybe it's ruled by Big Business, or Advertising, or a new Religious Order. It can be controlled by Mass Psychologists or Super-Criminals, or even

by Quiz-Masters. The ingenuity of our novelists and the logic of their chosen extrapolations are often very intriguing. But almost inevitably, they think of the future in terms of a military dictatorship, complete with force and espionage.

2. Secondly, we're apt to encounter something right out of the pages of our old friend Harriet Beecher Stowe—the UNDERGROUND. In some cases, it's actually a sort of Underground Railway, helping slaves to escape organized society. But mainly the Underground is presented as a revolutionary movement, governed within its own ranks by a totalitarian order as strict—or stricter—than the one it opposes. If anything, the typical science fiction Underground employs even more force and violence than the typical government of the future.

3. Thirdly, we find the dominance of FORCIBLE PSYCHOTHERAPEUTIC TECHNIQUES. Again and again we find "psychological warfare" entering the picture on a mass scale and—more drastically—on the individual level. Where would the science fiction novel of tomorrow be without "brain-washing"? Time and time again we find this convenient gambit used to alter the personality and outlook of the hero, the heroine or even the villain—as is the case in the finale of *The Demolished Man*. The masochistic concept is implicit; anybody can be "conditioned" to believe in anything, or react as desired. This is standard.

4. Also standard is the assumption that SCIENCE WILL GO ALONG WITH THE GAG and obediently wash brains for Capital, Labor, the Military, the Clergy or whatever group is posited as being in power. In fact, the whole fabric of all these novels hangs by a single thread — that scientists will always be willing to bend their backs over the washboard in a brain-laundry—that they will labor unthinkingly and unceasingly to produce new techniques, new technological advances and new weapons for the use of the group currently in authority.

5. This in turn seems to be based upon another standard assumption—that in the future, ECONOMIC INCENTIVE will still reign supreme. Oh, maybe they don't use old-fashioned currency any more, but everybody is still hot for "credits" or out to make a fast "megabuck."

6. Accepting these suppositions, it should come as no surprise that, in the great majority of those novels, it is blithely assumed that A VARIATION OF PRESENT-DAY "ANGLO-SAXON" CULTURE WILL CONTINUE TO RULE THE WORLD. Not the Asiatic, the Negro, the Russian or a miscegenated product; just little old us.

7. Furthermore, if the inhabitants of Earth ever reach other planets and discover life there, WE WILL COLONIZE AND RULE THE NATIVES. Our primary purpose, as always, will be economic exploitation of natural resources—or even unnatural resources, if we happen to find any.

8. The ultimate assumption, actually the sum total of all the rest, is simply that THE FUTURE HOLDS LITTLE BASIC CHANGE. Social relations and reactions, however disguised, will remain constant. Men and women will continue to like or dislike one another for their pulp-fiction, movie-melodrama, soap-opera attributes of "manliness" and "femininity." There will be reassuring evidence that "love" and "pride" and "virtue" do not change through the ages, and that, as the great eugenicist P. T. Barnum once pointed out, "There's one born every minute."

9. It is almost unnecessary to add a minor point which runs through these considerations: INDIVIDUALISM IS DEAD. The hero rebels, yes—but not to superimpose his own notions upon society; merely to restore the "normal" culture and value-standards of the mass-minds of the twentieth century. You won't find him fighting in defense of incest, homosexuality, free love, nihilism, the Single Tax, abolition of individual property-rights, euthanasia or the castration of the tonsils of Elvis Presley. Stripped right down to the bare

essentials, our hero just wants to kick the rascals out and put in a sound business administration. His viewpoint is that of today's average citizen: Godfrey-fearing, monogamous, and a firm believer in automatic wage-increases.

When we review these premises, we discover that most social criticism in science fiction novels is not directed against present-day society at all, as we may previously have assumed. Our authors, by and large, seem to believe wholly in the profit-incentive; in the trend to superimpose obedience and conformity by means of forcible conditioning; in the enduring liaison between the government, the military and scientists and technologists; in Anglo-Saxon cultural supremacy, if not necessarily outright "white supremacy"; in the sexual, aesthetic and religious mores of the day. Their criticism of the totalitarian states they envision is merely a matter of degree. They attempt to show the apparent dangers in allowing one group to "go a little too far"; actually, reduced to its essence, they merely echo Lord Acton's dictum that "Absolute power corrupts absolutely."

Hence the necessity of rebellion in the form of some sort of Underground movement. But this is always assumed to be just a temporary measure; ruthless because one must "fight fire with fire" and the ends justify the means. The implication is that once Law and Order are restored, everything will settle down to a general approximation of life as it is lived today — if not in actuality, at least in the pages of *Better Homes and Gardens*.

It is perhaps most surprising to contrast this unimaginative cultural viewpoint with the average science fiction novelist's technological viewpoint.

In technological extrapolation, our novelists have done, in many cases, an outstanding job. Men like Isaac Asimov, Arthur C. Clarke and George O. Smith have demonstrated great ingenuity in portraying the potentials and possibilities of our immediate futures. Robert A. Heinlein is praised, and rightfully so, for his abilities along these lines.

But what kind of people inhabit these Erewhons and Utopias, these gadget-glorified, scientifically-systematized civilizations? Let us consider an instance of what Mr. Heinlein
prophesies. And in order to be fair about it, let's confine
ourselves to an illustration of a benign social order, so we
won't attribute the actions of his characters to the fact that
they're supposed to be living under conditions of unnatural
tyranny.

Some years ago, in reviewing Heinlein's *Beyond This Horizon*, I made these observations, which I'll quote in part:

"In this novel, Robert A. Heinlein has done an outstanding
job of presenting 'adult' science fiction . . . a picture of life in
the twenty-third century, genetically controlled in an econo-
my of super-abundance.

"The protagonist is Hamilton Felix, a brilliant but erratic
inventor. The major plot details how he is persuaded to
father a child with the aid (psychological) of Genetics Mod-
erator Mordan and the assistance (physical) of his cousin,
Longcourt Phyllis. During the course of the tale he acts
in foiling a fascist revolt and helps in a scientific study of
metaphysical concepts. His child is enlisted in the study of
telepathy and the mysteries of life-after-death. Here Heinlein seems to realize how large a bite has been taken, and
wisely stops chewing.

"There is much more to this book, however, than the plot
outline would indicate. Avoiding the common pitfalls of
gadget description and mathematical expositions which pre-
occupy so many writers, Mr. Heinlein has chosen instead to
concentrate on the social philosophy of the future. Unfortunately, he cannot escape the subjectivity which permeates
every Utopian concept since More.

"Inevitably, the writer who deals in pseudo-prophecy must
remould the world nearer to his heart's desire. One cannot
escape the conviction that Heinlein's picture of life in the

future is based largely on wishful thinking and an exposition of personal philosophy. Whatever the cause, potential anachronisms abound. In a civilization based on scientifically controlled factors, Heinlein's citizens are given to carrying deadly weapons and shooting down total strangers for slight breaches in elaborate ceremonial courtesies. The incongruity of this conduct—learned dignitaries behaving like movie gangsters—mars credibility, despite the author's rationalization.

"Furthermore, in the midst of a society foundéd on highly organized patterns of social behavior, Heinlein's future men (bred—you must remember—for perfection and the elimination of undesirable traits) continue to guzzle beer, swill liquor, gamble wildly against rigged machines, lose their tempers instantly, and fall in love at first sight without rhyme or reason. A revival of football games also sweeps the world off its feet. Apparently, despite all the learned abracadabra of zygotes, genes, chromosomes and gametes, Mr. Heinlein still subscribes to a rather naive theory—'you can't change human nature.'

"And his concept of human nature, his concept of desirable attributes, seems to include pugnacity, sensuality and sentimentality in extremis. A survey of anthropology and ethnology might help him to revise his perspective, for human nature is not a constant, or even a clearly-demarcated concept, and human behavior can and does alter. Whole civilizations and cultures can exist and have existed without war or drug-addiction, and with every variant of patriarchal or matriarchal control. There is no more reason for supposing that "Anglish" modes are either superior or better fitted to survive than for one to believe that such well-established folkways as human sacrifice, public execution, slavery, religious prostitution, group suicide and marriage by capture are enduring manifestations of human nature. These phenomena have existed all over the world at various times throughout recorded history, and have played as important a part in the lives of millions of people as any of the social customs Heinlein chooses as desirable.*

"His single defense—'the fighting spirit has been preserved because it is biologically useful'—seems a complete rationalization. Since he has set up a world free from war, poverty or disease, free in most respects from social or commercial competition, the biological usefulness of his citizens shooting one another down in public lies open to question. It would seem much more logical, in Heinlein's genetically-controlled world, to esteem sexual virility and promote promiscuity and polygamy in an effort to advance mutations."

In justice to both Mr. Heinlein and myself, I must state that I concluded this review by saying, "But perhaps it is too much to expect of anyone to completely carry off such an ambitious project; it is not easy for man to play God and go Him one better by creating a world of utter perfection. Mr. Heinlein must be congratulated therefore on the basis of his accomplishments rather than criticized for his shortcomings. And his accomplishments, in the purely literary sense, are considerable. *Beyond This Horizon* is head and shoulders above the usual science fiction novel, both in conception and execution. Here is a book that belongs on the shelf of the thinking reader."

In subsequent correspondence with Heinlein concerning this book and his *Space Cadet*, we made the mutual discovery that our basic sociological views were not as far apart as we had first imagined. But the fact remains, when we attempt to view the average science fiction novel in terms of social criticism, we find that there is less here than meets the eye.

Our science fiction novelists, by and large, agree that dic-

---

* Diane Reinsberg reminds me, and justly so, that Mr. Heinlein has offered a wide latitude of variations in social organizations in many of his other works; thus demonstrating that he is by no means as arbitrary as I may have implied in my rather dated review. To which viewpoint I now offer fervent assent: in any discussion of this sort, after all the pros and cons are weighed, Heinlein rightfully emerges as a brilliant—rather than a horrible—example.

tators are bad—that a world run by and for Big Business is subject to false value-orientation—that religious bigotry or military fanaticism or criminal ethics are to be deplored as the basis of governmental philosophy. As social critics, then, they serve a function by showing how an extension of these tendencies in present-day society could bring about undesirable results in the future.

But there they seem, by and large, to stop. In presenting the dangers of possible future societies, they seem to be saying we need better government. Yet very few of them suggest that we need better citizens.

Consider some of the protagonists of our contemporary science fiction novels. Take a look at Ben Reich in *The Demolished Man*; the greedy aberrated Jean Valjean pursued by the future-day Javert, Lincoln Powell. Consider Gulliver Foyle, in Bester's more recent *Tiger! Tiger!* (*The Stars My Destination*). Gully Foyle is introduced to us as the same sort of character Eugene O'Neill chose as his hero in *The Hairy Ape*. Marooned in space in a freighter and enraged because another ship refuses to rescue him, Foyle escapes and plans vengeance against his enemies. In a matter of months he is transformed into a brilliant intellectual playboy, a marvelous scientist and technician, a supreme mass-psychologist, and he rebuilds his body as a miraculous fighting-machine. What does he do with these attributes and abilities? He commits rape, mayhem and murder. He lies, steals, cheats, assaults and cold-bloodedly tortures. Throughout the greater part of the book—which is distinguished by Bester's imaginative touches and artful styling—we are nevertheless confronted by a protagonist who behaves like a fiend in human and superhuman form. And the implied excuse for his conduct? Here is a hero who is out for revenge.

It isn't, in this instance, even so much that organized society in the future is labelled "wrong." It is merely that some members of that society have "wronged" our hero.

Consequently, he is permitted to indulge in every conceivable atrocity before he "reforms."

In Heinlein's recent effort, *The Door Into Summer*, we find a comparable situation on a much lesser scale. His hero is a distinguished engineer living in a rather pleasant, not-so-distant future. He too is double-crossed by associates. And the "plot" of the story, essentially, consists of how the hero manages to backtrack in time and return to revenge himself upon the evil-doers.

Did I mention "cops and robbers" some time ago, and "good guys and bad guys"? If so, it was with a purpose. Granted that the struggle between Good and Evil constitutes the basic drama of our literature, from the Scriptures on down—it is still well to question what, in these instances, constitutes "Good" and what is prefigured as "Evil."

From the standpoint of social criticism, the majority of today's science fiction novelists seem no more discriminating than that eminent literary figure, Mr. Michael Spillane.

They go to marvelously clever lengths to paint a convincing picture of a complex, intricately-ordered future society; complete, in many instances, with every technological advantage, and with the addition of super-psychotherapy, extrasensory perception, even teleportation powers.

But when it comes to a question of personal ethics, when it comes to a question of social justice—again and again we run right smack into our old friend Mike Hammer in disguise.

How, in this marvelous world of the future, does one go about settling an argument?

With the same old punch in the jaw . . . the same old kick in the guts . . . the same old bullet in the same old belly.

What is the proper motivating force for a hero? Greed for money, or "credits" . . . lust for power and control . . . or the desire for revenge.

Even if our hero starts out as the conformist member of a social order, behaving somewhat along the lines of an easy-going Jimmy Stewart, we can rest assured that midway in the novel he's going to turn into a facsimile of the late Humphrey Bogart.

His is the philosophy of pure Grab—he takes the money, the power, the girl and the law into his own hands.

Now this is not to say that all novels of "revenge" are necessarily poor ones. One need only remember *Moby Dick* —or on another level—*The Count of Monte Cristo*, for that matter.

But is "revenge" the only basis for heroic action? Or the thirst for domination, the need to usurp the roles of judge, jury and executioner?

The science fiction field has often been likened to a literary world in miniature. But one searches in vain through that world for a Jesus Christ . . . a Sydney Carton . . . a Philip Carey . . . or even a George Babbitt or a Leopold Bloom.

The common man is seldom the hero; if so, he doesn't remain common very long, but becomes a Key Figure. And the uncommon man is seldom presented as self-sacrificing; if he is dedicated to any cause greater than his own advancement—such as "freedom" in the abstract—we are generally given to understand that its triumph will find our hero getting a good snug berth down there in City Hall or on the Supreme Galactic Council.

Isaac Asimov recently pointed out that science fiction heroes are permitted to be intelligent. This is admirable. And yet, emotionally, most of them are primitive and immature.

Where is the science fiction novel with the ordinary family man as hero . . . or the teacher . . . or the creative artist . . . or the philosopher? Where is the science fiction novel that contents itself with showing us the everyday world of the future, devoid of Master Spies and Master Technicians and Master Psychologists and Master Criminals?

This is not to be considered a blanket denunciation. In fact, if you review what I have stated very carefully, you'll find that I haven't said a single word against blankets.

And you might also remember that I am not discussing these novels in terms of literary craftsmanship or entertainment. If so, I'd be the first to tell you how very much I enjoyed reading Damon Knight's vivid *Hell's Pavement*, Alfred Bester's *The Demolished Man* and Fritz Leiber's powerful *Gather, Darkness!*—the latter utilizing the standard picture of an authoritarian state but going far beyond the ordinary work in its criticism of Science as Religion. Here is fine writing, here are clever concepts, here is enthralling escape-fiction.

There are other exceptions which should be noted. *Brave New World*, of course—with social criticism as its primary and well-realized objective. We do get a touch of Big-Name dropping here, but by and large, Huxley presents a panoramic approach. Orwell's *1984* sticks to the common fate of the common man, with uncommon results. The common man also figures in Wilson Tucker's *The Long Loud Silence*. His hero's struggle to survive in the bomb-wasted and plague-infested wilderness is a moving, memorable and utterly logical adventure; what it has to say about man and motivations under conditions of stress is far more eloquent than a dozen science-fictional sermons served up with surrealistic shock-sequences. The same holds true for C. M. Kornbluth's *Not This August*; the old theme of totalitarian conquest takes on new meaning and new impact when told in terms of everyday living. In Frank M. Robinson's *The Power*, the author wisely adheres to familiar surroundings to stress the terrors of the unfamiliar. Damon Knight says that the novel is actually "anti-science fiction." This point is debatable, but even if we concede it, I'm sure that Knight admits Robinson's right to present this viewpoint as his own form of social criticism —and that he succeeded in producing a powerful, suspenseful book. There is fine theological philosophy to be found in Vercors' *You Shall Know Them*.

In Fredric Brown's *The Lights in the Sky Are Stars*, our hero is a 57-year-old rocket mechanic with an artificial leg. He and the heroine dedicate themselves to furthering a rocket flight to Jupiter. The heroine dies and the hero never makes the flight himself, but the thinking reader comes away from this book with at least a partial feeling of, "Yes, this is the way it will be—or could be." I repeat, the thinking reader; not the adolescent who wants to identify with a hero who is intent solely on smashing in the face of Authority.

At the other extreme, that of almost pure fantasy, we find such efforts as *Fahrenheit 451*, *War With the Newts* and *Doctor Arnoldi*. In *Fahrenheit 451*, Ray Bradbury has something to say about book-burning. Whether you agree with him or not, find his treatment convincing or unconvincing, or admire his highly personalized style (I do), there is nevertheless not the slightest doubt but that he has written a novel of social criticism in the science fiction field. In *War With the Newts* Karel Capek produced a remarkable satire, which fell flat on its face in this country twenty years ago, but has since been re-issued as a pocket-book. Here again is witty and perceptive social criticism. Such is also the case in Tiffany Thayer's early *Doctor Arnoldi*— in which the problems of overpopulation were discussed some twenty-five years before our learned ecologists and social scientists got around to becoming alarmed. And finally we have Theodore Sturgeon's *More Than Human*— a book that stands virtually alone in its consideration of empathy, the basic problem of MAN AGAINST HIMSELF, and even more important, MAN *FOR* HIMSELF and MAN *FOR* MANKIND.

Against the more popularly-held notions in the science fiction field that technology will save the world, or mass-psychological conditioning will save the world, these few dissenters stand, affirming that only man's spirit avails to save himself. They preach evolution rather than revolution, evaluation rather than revelation, individual right rather than individual might.

But does this mean, then, that only these few writers have performed a valuable function of social criticism and that all the rest are failures in this sense? Let us examine the actual relationship of the writer and society in order to find our answer.

Long ago, Walt Whitman wrote, "*To have great poets, there must be great audiences, too.*"

And in every attempt to judge an author's output, one must realize a basic truth: nothing is produced in a vacuum. It is so very easy, and so very convenient, for the average critic to chide the average author for not producing a masterpiece. But the average author needs an audience—and in today's world, the only way he can command that audience is through a commercial medium. In order to do so, he must produce something that will find favor with a publisher and an editor: the publisher and editor, in turn, must please the readers.

Great writers need great readers, and if science fiction novels have not, on the whole, offered more penetrating social criticism, it is largely because science fiction novel readers have not wanted it.

If a science fiction writer attempted to emulate Maugham with an *Of Extra-Terrestrial Bondage* or imitate Proust with a *Remembrance of Things Future*, the first people to stop him would be the editors and publishers—and this because they have no indication of a demand for this sort of reading material from their audience.

In the field of the short story, science fiction has found much greater latitude for expression of social attitudes and even antisocial attitudes. Other themes and other theses have been frequently advanced.

But we are considering the novels. Many of the authors of these novels have brilliantly demonstrated their ability to indulge in penetrating social criticism in their shorter efforts. One can only conclude that they modify their approach in the novel-form because the market is not there. And the market is not there because the readers are not there.

I myself have not published a science fiction novel of my own. And I am frank to say that if I ever do, the chances are greatly in favor of it being just such a book as many of these I have described here; complete with totalitarian state, active Underground, lone-hand hero and the usual Big Name trimmings. And I fully expect that even if I do my best to inject the element of social criticism, it will be editorially subordinated to so-called "entertainment" in the form of fast action, chase-sequences, gimmicks, gadgets, shock-value and all the rest. Like the majority of my fellow writers, I am wittingly or unwittingly mirroring my times.

For social criticism is not a spontaneous, self-generating phenomenon. *Uncle Tom's Cabin* was not the only, nor necessarily the best protest against slavery, according to many literary historians. Had it been published thirty years earlier, it might well have passed unnoticed — if indeed the book would have been written then in the first place. The social climate had to be right for the seed to be sown, to germinate, and to blossom forth in properly-cultivated soil.

The "protest" literature of the thirties has given way to the "hardboiled rugged individualism" of today—and while Cash McCall grabs the loot and Mike Hammer unravels the umbilicus with a bullet, one can hardly expect to find different attitudes or aspirations adumbrated in science fiction or any other field.

But is science fiction, therefore, failing in its function of social criticism?

Quite the contrary.

When a literature of imaginative speculation steadfastly adheres to the conventional outlook of the community regarding heroes and standards of values, it is indeed offering the most important kind of social criticism — unconscious social criticism.

With its totalitarian societies, its repudiation of individual activity in every role save that of the self-appointed leader and avenger, science fiction dramatizes the dilemma which torments modern man. It provides a very accurate mirror of our own problems, and of our own beliefs which fail to solve these problems.

Gazing into that mirror, we all might find it profitable to indulge in a bit of reflection.

INDEX

Acton, John Dalberg-, 110
Advent:Publishers, 47
Africa, 104
Ahab, Captain, 52
ALICE IN WONDERLAND, 40
Allen, Steve, 89
Alpha Centauri, 87
Amazing Stories, 79, 81
America—See: United States
American Federation of Labor, 85
American Medical Association, 100
ANIMAL FARM, 67
Anne of Austria, 107
Antarctic, the, 27
APE AND ESSENCE, 103
APOLOGIA, 47
Argus Books, 48
Aristotle, 12
Arlen, Michael, 39
ARROWSMITH, 8-9, 17
Asimov, Isaac, 28, 39, 47, 83, 110, 116
Astounding Science Fiction, 83
Austro-Hungarian Empire, 50
Austro-Hungarian Imperial Army, 50

BABBITT, 11, 51
Babbitt, George, 100, 116
Bacon, Francis, 92
Baffin Bay, 88
Bailey, J. O., 40, 48
Barnum, P. T., 109
Baum, L. Frank, 40
Behrman, S. N., 96
Bell, E. T., 47
Bell Telephone Laboratories, 34
Bellamy, Edward, 12
Benet, Stephen Vincent, 40

Berkeley, California, 25
Berlin, Irving, 93
Bester, Alfred, 10, 114, 117
Better Homes and Gardens, 110
BEYOND THIS HORIZON, 103, 111-113
Bible, the, 7, 115
BIG BALL OF WAX, THE, 103
Blair, Eric, 69
Bleiler, Everett F., 47
Blish, James, 76
Bloch, Robert, 11, 13
Bloom, Leopold, 116
BODY SNATCHERS, THE, 103
Bogart, Humphrey, 116
Boole, George, 57
Boston University, 28
Boucher, Anthony, 80, 83
BOY'S LIFE OF AL CAPONE, A, 98
Bradbury, Ray, 118
Bradley, Doctor, 96
BRAIN WAVE, 103
BRAVE NEW WORLD, 11, 40, 103, 104, 117
Bretnor, Reginald, 16, 31, 47, 48
BRING THE JUBILEE, 103
Bronx, New York, 78
Brooklyn, New York, 78
Brotherhood, the, 68
Brown, Fredric, 118
Brown University, 96
Budd, Lanny, 100
Buddha, Gautama, 44
Buddhism, Zen, 44
Budrys, A. J., 76
Burke, Kenneth, 56
Burton, Edmund, 58
Burton, Mary, 58
Byron, George Gordon, 12

Caesar, Julius, 54
CAINE MUTINY, THE, 40, 100
CALEB CATLUM'S AMERICA, 23
Calvinism, 51
Cambridge University, 67
Campbell, John W., Jr., 25, 47, 74, 79, 83
Capek, Karel, 39, 118
Carey, Philip, 116
Carroll, Lewis, 40
Carton, Sydney, 116
CASH MCCALL, 100
CAVES OF STEEL, THE, 39, 103
"Charlie Chan," 79
CHECKLIST OF FANTASTIC LITERATURE, THE, 47
Chicago, Illinois, 27, 35, 50, 98, 99
Childers, Erskine, 11
CHILDHOOD'S END, 102-103
Christian, Doctor, 105
Civil Defense, 101
CIVIL DISOBEDIENCE, 13
Clarke, Arthur C., 31, 40, 47, 73, 110
Clement, Hal, 39
Clooney, Rosemary, 82
Collier, John, 40
Columbia University, 78
"Coming Attraction," 16
Congress, U.S., 99
CONNECTICUT YANKEE IN KING ARTHUR'S COURT, A, 105
Constitution, U.S., 99
Coolidge, Calvin, 99
Cornog, Robert, 25
Correy, Lee, 28
COUNT OF MONTE CRISTO, THE, 116
Courtenay, Mitchell, 105
Coward-McCann, 47
Crane, Martin, 61-62
Crossgates, 69

da Vinci, Leonardo, 93
d'Artagnan, 107

Davenport, Basil, 65
Day, Don, 48
DAY OF THE TRIFFIDS, 102
de Bergerac, Cyrano, 32
de Camp, L. Sprague, 28, 29, 30, 40, 47
Defoe, Daniel, 20
del Rey, Evelyn, 76
del Rey, Lester, 39, 76
"Deluge at Norderney, The," 10
DEMOLISHED MAN, THE, 80, 90-91, 103, 108, 114, 117
Depression, the, 99
Derleth, August, 15
Dianetics, 83
Dinesen, Isak, 10
DOCTOR ARNOLDI, 103, 118
DOCTOR DOLITTLE, 98
Dodgson, Charles L., 40
DON QUIXOTE, 11, 50
Donnelly, Ignatius, 92
Dooley, Mr., 98
Doolittle, Alfred, 89
DOOMSDAY MEN, THE, 40
DOOR INTO SUMMER, THE, 103, 115
Dos Passos, John, 99
Dreiser, Theodore, 99
Dunne, Finley Peter, 98

Earth, 19, 59, 85, 101, 109
Eddison, E. R., 19
Edison, Thomas A., 92
Eich, the, 62
Einstein, Albert, 20
England, 11, 35, 56, 67, 68, 89
Ertz, Susan, 39
"Escape Into Space," 31f.
ESSAYS, 47
Eton, 67
EXECUTIVE SUITE, 100
"Experimental Approach to Dream Psychology Through Hypnosis, An," 76

FAHRENHEIT 451; 103, 118
FANCIES AND GOODNIGHTS, 40
Fantasy and Science Fiction, 14, 83
Far East, 87
Farber, Leslie H., 76
Farrell, James T., 99
FEMALE, THE, 40
Feuchtwanger, Lion, 23
Fire Island, New York, 80
Fisher, Charles, 76
Fisk University, 76
FLATLAND, 82
FLYING YORKSHIREMAN, THE, 19
FORBIDDEN AREA, 23
Ford Foundation, 66, 67
Fort Worth, Texas, 54
Fowler, H. W., 17
Foyle, Gulliver, 114-115
France, 89
Frank, Pat, 23, 40
FROM HERE TO ETERNITY, 43, 100
Funk & Wagnalls, 17

GABRIEL OVER THE WHITE HOUSE, 16
GADGET MAKER, THE, 23
Galactic Patrol series, 61-62
Galaxy Science Fiction, 80, 83
Garden of Eden, 12
GARGANTUA AND PANTAGRU-EL, 51
GATHER, DARKNESS!, 103, 117
Gautama Buddha, 44
GENERAL MANPOWER, 39
General Motors Corp., 100
Germany, 60, 67
Gernsback, Hugo, 79, 81, 106
GLADIATOR-AT-LAW, 103
God, 45, 65, 113
Goddard, Robert H., 34
Godfrey, Arthur, 89, 110
Gold, Horace L., 79-80, 83

GOLDEN ASS, THE, 65
GOLDEN KAZOO, THE, 103
GOOD SOLDIER SCHWEIK, THE, 50, 59
Grahame, Kenneth, 40
GRAPES OF WRATH, THE, 20
"Gravy Planet," 72
GRAY LENSMAN, 19
GREAT CRYPTOGRAM, THE, 92
GREENER THAN YOU THINK, 103, 105
Griffith, Maxwell, 23
Gulliver, Lemuel, 55-56
GULLIVER'S TRAVELS, 11, 55-59

Hairy Ape, The, 114
Hale, Edward Everett, 32
Hamilton, Edmond, 30-31
Hamilton Felix, 111
Hamlet, 32
Hamlet, 81
Hammer, Mike, 115, 120
Harrison, Rex, 82
Hasek, Jaroslav, 50
Hedy, 73
Heinlein, Robert A., 8-9, 11, 70, 83, 90, 91, 110-113, 113f., 115
HELL'S PAVEMENT, 103, 105, 117
Henry VIII, 35
Hepburn, Audrey, 82
HIGHWAYS IN HIDING, 103
HOLD BACK THE NIGHT, 40
Holiday, 80
Houyhnhnms, the, 58
HUCKSTERS, THE, 20
HUMANOIDS, THE, 103
Humpty Dumpty, 15
Huxley, Aldous, 12, 40, 117
Huxley, T. H., 47
Hygeia, 100

I AM THINKING OF MY DAR-LING, 40, 103

IN SEARCH OF WONDER, 47, 75
INDEX TO THE SCIENCE FICTION
    MAGAZINES, *1926-1950*; 48
Industrial Worker, The, 72
Industrial Workers of the World, 72
Ishmael, 52
IT CAN'T HAPPEN HERE, 16, 39
Italy, 60, 89

Javert, 114
Jesus Christ, 116
Jones, James, 43
Jourdain, M., 9
Joyce, James, 42, 79
JUNGLE, THE, 35, 50, 59, 63
Jupiter, 118
Justinian I, 39

Kafka, Franz, 85
Kantor, MacKinlay, 40
Kepler, Johannes, 32
Kildare, Doctor, 105
Knight, Damon, 15, 47, 56, 74, 75,
    76, 105, 117
Knight, Eric, 19
Knox, Ronald, 7-8
Kornbluth, Cyril M., 8, 10-11, 39,
    83-84, 117
Kornbluth, Mary, 76
Korzybski, Alfred, 47
Kuttner, Henry, 83, 90

Lafferty, Perry, 81
Laputa, 57-58
Lardner, Ring, 98
LAST AND FIRST MEN, 65
LAST HURRAH, THE, 100
LAST MEN IN LONDON, THE, 65
Latham, Philip, 28
Legree, Simon, 51
Leiber, Fritz, 16, 117
Leibnitz, Gottfried Wilhelm von, 57

Leinster, Murray, 28
Lensmen, 62
LEST DARKNESS FALL, 40
Lewis, C. S., 20, 32, 40
Lewis, Sinclair, 8, 16, 17, 39, 51, 99,
    100
Ley, Willy, 24, 29, 31, 47
LIGHTS IN THE SKY ARE STARS,
    THE, 103, 118
Lilliput, 56-57
LIMBO, 103, 105
Lincoln, Abraham, 50
London, England, 32, 33, 69
LONG LOUD SILENCE, THE, 62-
    65, 103, 105, 117
LONG REMEMBER, 40
Longcourt Phyllis, 111
Lovecraft, H. P., 60
LOVERS, THE, 103
Lucian of Samosata, 32

McCall, Cash, 120
McCall's Magazine, 80, 86
McCann, Edson, 105
McCarthy, Joseph R., 99
McHugh, Vincent, 23, 40
*Magazine of Fantasy and Science Fic-
    tion, The*, 14, 83
MAGIC, INC., 19
Main Street, 100
Malone, Young Doctor, 105
MAN IN THE GRAY FLANNEL
    SUIT, THE, 100
Manhattan Island, New York, 78
MAN'S MORTALITY, 39
Marconi, Guglielmo, 92
Mars, 19, 30, 37, 57, 87, 106
Martin, John S., 39
Martine, Doctor, 105
Marxism, 59
Massachusetts Institute of Technol-
    ogy, 25
Matheson, Richard, 74
Maugham, W. Somerset, 119

Maywood, Illinois, 98
Melville, Herman, 52-54
MEN LIKE GODS, 12
Mencken, H. L., 98-99
Merriam-Webster, 17
MESSIAH, 103, 105
Michigan Boulevard, 54
"Midnight, Forecastle," 52
Milky Way, 31, 32
Miller, Henry, 42
Ministry of Love, 70
"Misfit," 30
MOBY DICK, 52-54, 116
Moby Dick, 52
MODERN ENGLISH USAGE, 17
MODERN SCIENCE FICTION: ITS
  MEANING AND ITS FUTURE,
  47
MOLL FLANDERS, 20
Montgomery, Robert, 81
Moore, Ward, 105
Moravia, Alberto, 42
Mordan Claude, 111
More, St. Thomas, 111
MORE THAN HUMAN, 103, 118
Morris, William, 12
Morse, Samuel F. B., 92
Moskowitz, Sam, 14

NEEDLE, 39
NERVES, 39
New York, New York, 33, 54, 72, 78
New Yorker, The, 71
Newgate Street, 58
Newton, Isaac, 34
"Nick Carter," 79
NINETEEN EIGHTY-FOUR, 11, 39,
  66-71, 103, 104, 106, 117
Nolan, Lewis, 58
North Sea, 11
NOT AS A STRANGER, 100
NOT THIS AUGUST, 39, 103, 117
Nuremberg, Germany, 66
NUTRO 29; 103

Oberth, Hermann, 31, 34
O'Brien, 68-69
ODD JOHN, 39-40, 65, 103
OF EXTRA-TERRESTRIAL BOND-
  AGE, 119
Okies, 99
Oliver, Chad, 28
"On Taking Science Fiction Serious-
  ly," 48
O'Neill, Eugene, 114
Orwell, George, 12, 39, 66-71, 106,
  117
OUT OF THE DEEPS, 102
OUT OF THE SILENT PLANET, 20,
  40
Oxford University, 7-8
Oz series, 19, 98

Parsons, Tom, 67
PEBBLE IN THE SKY, 39
Peenemuende, Germany, 31-33
Pequod, 52
Perri Press, 48
PILGRIMS THROUGH SPACE AND
  TIME, 40, 48
Pip, 52-53
PLAYER PIANO, 103, 105
Poe, Edgar Allan, 32
Pohl, Frederik, 72-73, 76
Popular Mechanics, 26
Powell, Lincoln, 114
POWER, THE, 103, 117
PREFERRED RISK, 103, 105
PRELUDE TO SPACE, 40
Presley, Elvis, 109
Priestley, J. B., 40
Prohibition, 99
Proteus, Paul, 105
Proust, Marcel, 119
Providence, Rhode Island, 96
Pshush-Maker, the, 88
Psychoanalytic Quarterly, 76
PUPPET MASTERS, THE, 102
PYGMALION, 89

QUO VADIS, 32

Rabelais, Francois, 51
Randlett, Samuel, 76
Rarey, John S., 58
Reich, Ben, 114
Reinsberg, Diane, 113f.
REMEMBRANCE OF THINGS FU-
TURE, 119
REPRIEVE FROM PARADISE, 103
REVOLT IN 2100; 103
Rhode Island, 96
RIDDLE OF THE SANDS, THE, 11
Robinson, Frank M., 117
Rock, The, 78
Rogers, Will, 90, 99
Room 101; 70-71
Rousseau, Jean Jacques, 58
Royal Society, the, 59
Russia, 60, 67

S., H., 31f.
Sagan, Francoise, 42
St. Clement's, 68
St. John's College, 78
Samosata, Lucian of, 32
SANGAREE, 23
"Sargasso of Space, The," 30
Sartre, Jean-Paul, 42
Saturday Review, The, 31f.
SCIENCE AND SANITY, 47
Science Fiction Advertiser, The, 48
Scoles, A. B., 30
Scriptures, 115
Seacoast Bohemia, 19
Seaton, Dorothy, 60
Seaton, Richard, 60-62
SECRET MASTERS, THE, 103
"Secret Service," 84-85
SEVEN FAMOUS NOVELS, 39
"Shadow, The," 79
Shakespeare, William, 92
Shasta Publishers, 47

Shaw, George Bernard, 89
Shoreditch, 69
SHRINKING MAN, THE, 74
Sinclair, Upton, 35, 50, 63, 99, 100
Single Tax, 109
SINISTER BARRIER, 102
SIRIUS, 65
SKYLARK OF SPACE, THE, 13
Skylark series, 59-62
Slaughter, Frank G., 23
Sloane, William, 39
Slobbovia, 87
Smith, Edward E., 19, 20, 28, 47,
59-62, 64, 83, 104
Smith, George O., 28, 110
Smith, Harrison, 31f.
Smith, Lady, 7-8
Smith, Winston, 68-71
Socrates, 47
"Solution Unsatisfactory," 25
SPACE CADET, 103, 113
SPACE MERCHANTS, THE, 72-74,
103, 105
Sparta, 60
Spillane, Mickey, 15, 115
Square, A., 82
Squinka, 80
Standard Magazines, 79
Stapledon, Olaf, 32, 40, 65-66
STARMAKER, 65
STARS MY DESTINATION, THE,
80, 103, 114-115
Steinbeck, John, 20, 99
Stewart, James, 116
Stine, G. Harry, 31, 47
Stowe, Harriet Beecher, 50, 98, 108
Stuart, Don A., 28
Sturgeon, Theodore, 15, 83, 90, 91,
118
SUCCESS, 23
"Such, Such Were the Joys," 68-69
Superman Comics, 79
Swift, Jonathan, 56-58
SWORD IN THE STONE, THE, 40
SYNDIC, THE, 103

Taine, John, 23, 28
TAKEOFF, 39
Texas, 54
Thayer, Tiffany, 118
THIRTEEN O'CLOCK, 40
THIS FORTRESS WORLD, 103
Thoreau, Henry David, 13
Thorndike-Barnhart, 17
Thought Police, 69
THREE MUSKETEERS, THE, 107
Tide, 72
TIGER! TIGER!, 103, 114-115
TIME MACHINE, THE, 102
TIME STREAM, THE, 23
TO WALK THE NIGHT, 39
TOMORROW, 23
Tucker, Wilson, 62-65, 105, 117
Turner, Harold R., 29
Twain, Mark, 98, 105
Tweed, Thomas F., 16
TWENTY THOUSAND LEAGUES UNDER THE SEA, 102

ULYSSES, 79
UNCLE TOM'S CABIN, 11, 50, 59, 63, 120
United States Air Force, 31
United States of America, 31, 32, 51, 54, 77, 78, 89, 99
University College, 7, 14f., 49f., 77f., 97f.
University of Chicago, 7, 14f., 25, 49f., 77f., 78, 97f.
University of Pennsylvania, 78

Valjean, Jean, 114
Valley Forge, Pennsylvania, 37
van Doren, Charles, 78
van Vogt, A. E., 83, 90
Vercors, 117
Verne, Jules, 28, 29, 32, 81, 103
Vidal, Gore, 105

Vienna, Austria, 89
von Braun, Wernher, 31

Wakeman, Frederic, 20
WAKING WORLD, 65
WALDO, 24-27
WAR OF THE WORLDS, THE, 13
WAR WITH THE NEWTS, THE, 39, 103, 118
Washington, George, 37
Waugh, Evelyn, 63
Wellman, Manly Wade, 80
Wellman, Paul, 40
Wells, H. G., 12, 28, 32, 39, 81, 102, 103
West, Anthony, 71
Westinghouse Electric Corp., 34
White Sands Proving Ground, 29
White, T. H., 40
White, William A. P., 47
Whitman, Walt, 119
"Who Goes There?" 74
WILD TALENT, 103
Wilde, Oscar, 29
Winchell, Paul, 79, 80
WIND IN THE WILLOWS, THE, 40
WIZARD OF OZ, THE, 40
Wobblies, 72
WOMAN ALIVE, 39
WORLD BELOW, THE, 40
World War II, 29, 33, 100, 101
WORM OUROBOROS, THE, 19
Wouk, Herman, 40
Wright, Orville and Wilbur, 93
Wright, S. Fowler, 40
Wylie, Philip, 23, 28, 32, 101

YOU SHALL KNOW THEM, 103, 117

Zen Buddhism, 44
Zlxxt, 19